EZRA POUND
and the Troubadour Tradition

Princeton Essays in Literature

Advisory Committee: Robert Fagles,
Claudio Guillen, Robert Maguire,
Theodore Ziolkowski

For a listing of all titles, see page 161.

Stuart Y. McDougal

EZRA POUND
and the Troubadour Tradition

PRINCETON UNIVERSITY PRESS
Princeton, New Jersey

L.C. Card: 72-2575
I.S.B.N.: 0-691-06236-6

Publication has been aided by the Whitney Darrow
Publication Reserve Fund of Princeton University Press

This book has been composed in Linotype Janson

Printed in the United States of America
by Princeton University Press,
Princeton, New Jersey

Second Printing, 1974

For Menakka

Acknowledgments

The topic for this study was initially suggested by Daniel Hoffman, who carefully supervised the work in its early stages as a Ph.D. dissertation. M. Roy Harris taught me Provençal in classrooms at the University of Pennsylvania where the spirit of Ezra Pound still lurked. I am very grateful to both for their encouragement and criticism.

I also wish to thank John Peck, Robert Fagles, A. Walton Litz, and Hugh Kenner for their helpful suggestions.

The Provençal texts quoted in this study are those which were accessible to Pound.

Excerpts from the following published works of Ezra Pound are reprinted by permission of New Directions Publishing Corporation, New York and Faber & Faber, London.

The Cantos: Copyright 1934, 1937, 1940, 1948, 1956, 1968 by Ezra Pound; *Personae*: Copyright 1926 by Ezra Pound; *A Lume Spento and Other Early Poems*: Copyright 1965 by Ezra Pound and New Directions Publishing Corporation; *Translations*: Copyright 1926, 1954, 1963 by Ezra Pound; *The Literary Essays*: Copyright 1918, 1920, 1934 by Ezra Pound; *The ABC of Reading*, Copyright 1934 by Ezra Pound; *The Letters of Ezra Pound, 1907-1941*, edited by D. D. Paige, Copyright 1950.

Provenca, Canzoni, Exultations, *"I Gather the Limbs*

ACKNOWLEDGMENTS

of Osiris": All Rights Reserved. Reprinted by permission of New Directions Publishing Corporation for Dorothy Pound, Committee for Ezra Pound, and Faber & Faber, London.

The Spirit of Romance: All Rights Reserved. Reprinted by permission of New Directions Publishing Corporation and Peter Owen, Ltd., London.

Abbreviated Titles by Which Ezra Pound's Works Are Cited

P   *Personae* (New Directions, 1971).
SR   *The Spirit of Romance* (New Directions, 1953).
LE   *The Literary Essays of Ezra Pound*, edited and with an introduction by T. S. Eliot (New Directions, 1954).
GB   *Gaudier-Brzeska: A Memoir* (New Directions, 1970).
C   *Canzoni* (London, 1911).
Pr   *Provença* (Boston, 1910).
L   *The Letters of Ezra Pound, 1907-1941*, edited by D. C. Paige (New York, 1950).
ABC   *ABC of Reading* (New Directions, 1960).
ALS   *A Lume Spento and Other Early Poems* (New Directions, 1965).
T   *The Translations of Ezra Pound*, with an introduction by Hugh Kenner (New Directions, 1963).

Table of Contents

EZRA POUND
and the Troubadour Tradition

Introduction

THE POSSIBILITIES OF PROVENCE

Breathing I draw the air to me
Which I feel coming from Provença,
All that is thence so pleasureth me
That whenever I hear good speech of it
I listen laughing and straightway
Demand for each word an hundred
So fair to me is the hearing.
> Peire Vidal, "Ab l'alen tir
> vas me l'aire," translated by
> Ezra Pound, c. 1910

In the autumn of 1904, Ezra Pound began his studies of Provençal at Hamilton College under Dr. William Pierce Shepherd. In March of the following year, he wrote his mother that his "extra work" for the following semester would be "with Bill Shepherd . . . in Provençal, 'The Troubadours of Dante.' "[1] Two months later, he published his first translation from Provençal in the *Hamilton Literary Magazine*. This early interest was to become an abiding one for Pound, as his recent cantos show.

Pound was extremely fortunate in being able to study under as distinguished a scholar as Dr. Shepherd at a time when Provençal studies were flourishing. After graduat-

[1] Yale Letters 39, March 1905. Quoted in Thomas H. Jackson, *The Early Poetry of Ezra Pound* (Cambridge, 1968), p. 248.

3

ing from Hamilton College (1891), Shepherd had studied at the University of Grenoble, the Sorbonne, and the University of Heidelberg; thus he was exposed to the revival of interest in Provençal taking place in France and Germany during this period. In the fifty years preceding Pound's graduation from Hamilton, close to thirty editions of individual Provençal poets were published, in addition to seven grammars and dictionaries (including Levy's monumental *Provenzalisches Supplement-Wörterbuch*) and several anthologies.[2] Nor was the interest in Provençal studies limited to the continent. In England a number of popularized studies appeared; notably Francis Hueffer's *The Troubadours: A History of Provençal Life and Literature in the Middle Ages* (1878), Ida Farnell's *The Lives of the Troubadours* (1896), and H. J. Chaytor's *The Troubadours of Dante* (1902). Pound was familiar with all of the English studies and many of the European ones.

Pound's early interest in Provençal poetry reflects that of the scholars and editors whose works he had studied. In their view Provence was the first culture in Western Europe to produce a literature in the vernacular,[3] and thus an examination of Provençal poetry was a return to origins. Indeed, the influence of Provençal poetry on the lyric poetry of Spain, Portugal, Northern France (les *Trouvères*), Italy (the *dolce stil nuovo*), Germany (the minnesingers), and England was considerable,[4] and an

[2] A good bibliography of Provençal studies prior to 1912 is available in H. J. Chaytor, *The Troubadours* (Cambridge, 1912), pp. 141-144.

[3] More recently scholars have discovered some Hispano-Arabic poetry that antedates it.

[4] See, for example: J. Audiau, *Les Troubadours et l'Angleterre* (Paris, 1927); G. Bertoni, *I Trovatori d'Italia* (Modena, 1915);

understanding of any modern European poetry would be incomplete without some knowledge of Provençal poetry. It is appropriate that Pound began his career by translating the first known Provençal poem—a refrain to a Latin song. As he has stated repeatedly, the young poet, like the scientist, "begins by learning what has been discovered already" (*LE*, 6:1913), and "any study of European poetry is unsound if it does not commence with a study of that art in Provence" (*LE*, 101:1913). Thus, in terms of Pound's constant search for "inventors" and "origins," Provence has played an important role.

However, Pound goes far beyond the interests of most nineteenth century scholars in his insistence upon the contemporaneity of certain medieval values. These values are apparent in Pound's early translations, which are chosen for thematic reasons. These translations serve as "masks" for the poet, as he speaks through the persona of a Bertran de Born or a Peire Bremon lo Tort. They are also important technical exercises: in them, Pound is confronted with the problem of finding a suitable form and language to convey the experience of the Provençal. Here too Pound has moved away from the work of his predecessors, for his translations become increasingly interpretative and less literal. He condenses, deletes, and expands, and the result in each instance is a highly original work. Pound has helped redefine our concept of what a translation can and should be, and he is therefore largely

---

H. J. Chaytor, *The Troubadours of Dante* (Oxford, 1902); V. Crescini, ed., *Provenza e Italia: Studi* (Firenze, 1930); I. Frank, *Trouvères et Minnesänger: Recueil de Textes Pour Servir à l'Etude des Rapports Entre la Poésie Lyrique Romane et le Minnesang au XIIᵉ siècle* (Saarbrücken, 1952) and K. Vossler, "Die Dichtung der Trobadors und ihre Europäische Wirkung," *Romanische Forschungen*, LI (1937), pp. 253-278.

responsible for the great renaissance of poetic translation that has taken place in this century.

Pound's Provençal personae are closely related to his translations. Both, as he has stated, serve as "masks of the self" (*GB*, 85). Through these poetic re-creations of historical characters he is able to explore alien sensibilities whose qualities are relevant to the modern world. Even the earliest of these personae is the mixture of "fact" and "fiction" that he continued to manipulate in "Near Perigord" and later in *The Cantos*. He views each of these studies as an interpretative "key" to the life and works of the poet being presented. Thus, through Pound, we discover the "real" Arnaut de Mareuil, and the "real" Peire Vidal. Their "reality" reveals a great deal about the ideals Pound respects, for, taken together, the Provençal personae define the qualities of this culture which Pound has found attractive and which he has made a permanent part of his own world. This is especially true of what he conceives to be the love ethic of Provence. Although certain aspects of this ethic are present in his early work, it does not become clearly defined until 1910-1912. At this time Pound was immersed in early Tuscan poetry, especially that of Cavalcanti. Here he discovered a way of presenting the lady that was implicit in much Provençal poetry. Pound worked backwards from Tuscan poetry to the origins of the idealization of the lady in Provençal poetry; from this point onward this attitude became his own.

Through his work with Provence, Pound acquired themes and techniques that have become an important part of his total *oeuvre*. He moves from literal translations through inventive translations to original poems that develop Provençal themes and utilize Provençal forms. Pound creates a new language to express the unified sensibility of medieval Provence and thereby affirms the importance of this sensibility to the modern world. By making the spirit of Provence his own, Pound has shown us that it is a living culture, with a vitality and importance we cannot ignore.

Chapter I

THE SEARCH FOR A LANGUAGE:
Early Translations

Ma qui la morta poesi risurga
> Dante, *Purgatorio*, I, 7.
> Pound, Epigraph to "Canzoniere"

For three years, out of key with his time,
He strove to resuscitate the dead art
Of poetry . . .

> *Hugh Selwyn Mauberley*

THE act of translation has had a dual function for Pound: it has helped him develop technically as a poet and it has provided him with a series of "complete masks of the self" (*GB*,85). The translations are thus important exercises by which Pound has enriched his resources in trying to find equivalents for other poems in his own language. "Poetic translation," George Steiner has noted, "plays a unique role inside the translator's own speech. It drives inward. Anyone translating a poem, or attempting to, is brought face to face, as by no other exercise, with the genius, bone-structure and limitations of his native tongue. . . . Translation taxes and thus makes inventory of our resources."[1] In his early translations Pound is seeking a suitable form of English for Provençal poetry, and, in the process, both developing as an American poet and

[1] George Steiner, ed., *The Penguin Book of Modern Verse Translation* (Middlesex, 1966), p. 27.

8

altering our notions of what a translation should be. Moreover, translation is a way of penetrating an alien sensibility and culture and making it one's own: thus the poet dons a series of masks, as he becomes for a moment Arnaut de Mareuil and then Peire Vidal. It is, as we shall see, a very short step from this conception of translation and this type of imitation to the development of the persona in "Marvoil," "Na Audiart," or "Sestina: Altaforte."

Pound's entire corpus of translations also constitutes an act of criticism: his very choice of poems reveals a critical attitude. Pound defines this selection as "excernment: The general ordering and weeding out of what has actually been performed. The elimination of repetitions. The work analogous to that which a good hanging committee or a curator would perform in a National Gallery or in a biological museum" (*LE*, 75:1934).

The period from 1908-1910 is an extraordinarily rich one in translations from Provençal: during these two years Pound translated, in part or whole, nearly fifty poems representing the major works of all the important troubadour poets. Well over half of these were published in *The Spirit of Romance* (1910); they are mostly the results of Pound's teaching at The Polytechnic, a school in London, and are what he called "merely exegetic" translations (*SR*, 106). The others, published in *Personae* (1909) and *Exultations* (1909), show Pound "substituting verse in one language for verse in another" (*SR*, 106). These are Pound's first attempts at poetic translation, and he is groping towards a suitable English equivalent of Provençal, as well as trying to come to terms with the Provençal verse forms. Although these attempts are largely unsuccessful (Pound eliminated all but one of these poems from his *Personae* of 1926), they helped Pound to define his interest in Provençal culture,

9

and greatly aided him in his growth as a poet forging a language for himself in English.

One of Pound's earliest published works is the translation of a Latin poem with a refrain in Provençal. The refrain was long considered the first known example of a Provençal poem.[2] For Pound it was a pleasant coincidence that the first Provençal poem was a dawn song since he viewed the Middle Ages as a period of awakening, rather than as the "dark ages." Chapter I of *The Spirit of Romance* is called "The Phantom Dawn"; this title refers to the Latin literature that Pound considered "a foreboding of the spirit which was, in great part, to be characteristic of the literature of the Middle Ages" (*SR*, 12). The poem Pound translates represents the moment of transition between these two literatures: "The stanzas of the song have been written down in Latin, but the refrain remains in the tongue of the people" (*SR*, 11):

> L alba par umet mar atras el poy
> Pas abigil miraclar Tenebris.[3]
>
> [Dawn draws the sun over the humid sea
> Then the vigil passes, the shadows brighten.][4]

Pound first published this poem in the May 1905 issue of the *Hamilton Literary Magazine*, under the title of "Belangal Alba":[5]

[2] In *Eos: an inquiry into the theme of lovers' meetings and partings at dawn in poetry*, ed. A. T. Hatto (London, 1965), B. Woledge states that "we cannot understand . . . [the poem's] refrain and we are not even sure to what Romance dialect it belongs" (p. 354). See also pages 77 and 272.

[3] Text in Ezra Pound, *Personae* (London, 1909), p. 59.

[4] All translations in brackets are my own.

[5] Quoted in Charles Norman, *Ezra Pound* (New York, 1969), p. 12.

10

Phoebus shineth e'er his glory flyeth,
   Aurora drives faint light athwart the land,
And the drowsy watcher cryeth,
                    "Arise!"

Ref:

Dawn light, o'er sea and height, riseth bright,
Passeth vigil, clear shineth on the night.

They be careless of the gates, delaying,
   Whom the ambush glides to hinder
Whom I warn and cry to, praying,
                    "Arise!"

Ref:

O'er cliff and ocean white dawn appeareth,
Passeth vigil, and the shadows cleareth.

Forth from our Arcturus, North Wind bloweth
   Stars of heaven sheathe their glory
And, Sun-driven, forth-goeth
                  Settentrion.

Ref:

O'er sea-mist and mountain is dawn display'd,
It passeth watch and maketh night afraid.

Notice that the refrain, which is repeated without change in the original poem, is translated in three different ways. Even in his first translation, Pound felt free to modify the original text. The reader is aware of the way the refrain modulates a given theme, and the changes in each refrain are quite successful. By creating a speaker in the second stanza, Pound personalizes the poem, although the meaning is in no way clarified by this change. The archaic

11

diction further obscures the sense of the translation, and makes the work a period piece. Because of textual problems it is virtually impossible to know whether to consider the poem a hymn or a secular song, although Pound's version favors the latter. The tension between religious and secular imagery becomes one of the characteristic features of the great Provençal *albas* that follow.

Pound republished this poem four years later in *Personae*, under the title "Alba Belingalis," with a few minor changes.[6] A third version of the refrain appeared in *The Spirit of Romance* a year later, and although Pound dropped this poem from *Personae* (1926), it had an obvious importance—both historic and literary—for him. The *alba*, with its ambiguous treatment of the dawn as an end to the adulterous night of pleasure and the beginning of a new day, and its tension between secular and religious values, plays an important part in Pound's total interpretation of Provençal culture, especially in his "Homage à la Langue d'Oc." *A Lume Spento* (1908) contains "That Pass Between the False Dawn and the True," and "To the Dawn: Defiance," in which the night is not adulterous but associated with dream and unreality. *A Quinzaine for This Yule* (1908) is dedicated to "The Aube of the West Dawn," and includes "Aube of the West Dawn: Venetian June." Thus, from the very beginning of his career Pound was intrigued by the implications of this *genre*.

Exultations (1909) contains a translation of another famous *alba*, the anonymous "En un vergier sotz fuella d'albespi," which Pound entitled "Alba Innominata":

> In a garden where the whitethorn spreads her
> leaves

[6] Pound drops the first version of the refrain, and repeats the second in its place. The other changes are mainly typographical.

12

My lady hath her love lain close beside her,
Till the warder cries the dawn—Ah dawn that
    grieves!
Ah God! Ah God! That dawn should come so soon!

"Please God that night, dear night should never
    cease,
Nor that my love should parted be from me,
Nor watch cry 'Dawn'— Ah dawn that slayeth peace!
Ah God! Ah God! That dawn should come so soon!

"Fair friend and sweet, thy lips! Our lips again!
Lo, in the meadow there the birds give song!
Ours be the love and Jealousy's the pain!
Ah God! Ah God! That dawn should come so soon!

"Sweet friend and fair take we our joy again
Down in the garden, where the birds are loud,
Till the warder's reed astrain
Cry God! Ah God! That dawn should come so soon!

"Of that sweet wind that comes from Far-Away
Have I drunk deep of my Belovéd's breath,
Yea! of my Love's that is so dear and gay.
Ah God! Ah God! That dawn should come so soon!"

Envoi

Fair is this damsel and right courteous,
And many watch her beauty's gracious way.
Her heart toward love is no wise traitorous.
Ah God! Ah God! That dawns should come so soon!

Pound has retained the outward form of the poem, with
six stanzas, each containing four lines of ten syllables, the
last line of each stanza being a refrain including the word

13

alba, a distinctive feature of this *genre*. He has modified the aaaB rhyme scheme to abaC (the capital letter indicates that the same word is repeated from stanza to stanza), a form that is obviously less demanding. In terms of the content, Pound has made some significant alterations. In the Provençal version the first stanza is spoken by an anonymous speaker who narrates the scene from afar and summarizes the entire situation in three lines:

> En un vergier sotz fuella d'albespi
> tenc la dompna son amic costa si,
> tro la gayta crida que l'alba vi.[7]

> [In a garden under the hawthorne's leaves
> A lady held her love close to her
> Until the look-out cries that he's seen
>   the dawn.]

By translating "la dompna" as "my lady," Pound has made the anonymous narrator the male participant, thus giving his poem an immediacy lacking in the original. But the effects of this change are even more far-reaching, because it alters the way in which we read the last stanza (and ultimately the entire poem). In the Provençal version, stanza 6, which Pound calls an "envoi," is also spoken by the narrator of stanza 1. Having quoted the lady at some length (stanzas 2-5) as she chronicles in detail her adulterous night, the narrator speaks directly to her, and his words (translated quite literally by Pound) are a eulogy of the woman's beauty and virtue. This is striking precisely because the narrator is *not* involved in what he is describing, but is an impartial witness. Notice the terms

[7] Text in Carl Appel, *Provenzalische Chrestomathie* (Leipzig, 1895), p. 90.

of his praise. The lady's "beutat" is more than physical: it represents a sort of moral perfection, and thus her nocturnal liaison is viewed as a very natural and even positive thing. This, in effect, confirms the woman's description of her lover (stanza 5) as the epitome of certain courtly virtues. In the Provençal he is "handsome, courtly, and gay" ("belh e cortes e gay"): Pound's version is much weaker, for "dear and gay" lack the moral force of the original. Pound realizes the necessity of maintaining a distance between stanzas 5 and 6, and by calling stanza 6 an "envoi" he sees to it that we do not confuse this speaker with the speaker (identified by him as the lover) of stanza 1. In both versions the participants in stanzas 2-5 epitomize many of the best aspects of this society.

Pound also alters the nature of the experience related by the lady. In both poems the physical setting is idyllic, resembling in outward appearance a bountiful Garden of Eden. God is invoked, not only in the refrain, but in the lady's opening words. The physical aspect of love, treated rather delicately (although unequivocally) in the Provençal version, is emphasized in Pound's translation. For example, line 9 of the Provençal reads "Beautiful gentle friend, let us kiss, you and I," which Pound translates as "Fair friend and sweet, thy lips! Our lips again," which is reminiscent of one of Dowson's dying falls. In fact, one is struck here, as in Pound's translation of the earlier *alba*, by the mixture of Pre-Raphaelite and *fin-de-siècle* diction which abounds: this tone is supported by the languid expressions "Ah dawn that grieves!" (l. 3) and "Ah dawn that slayeth peace!" (l. 7), two interpolations that have no basis whatsoever in the Provençal text. Archaisms such as "damsel" for "dompna" ("lady") and "right courteous" for "agradans" ("agreeable") contribute to this tone.[8]

Moreover, Pound de-emphasizes the theme of adultery, around which the Provençal poem (and the entire *genre*) turns. Line 12 of the Provençal reads "Let us do everything in spite of the jealous one (*gilos*)" who quite clearly is the woman's husband and even possibly, as James J. Wilhelm suggests, the " 'jealous God' (*Deus zelotes*) of the Old Testament."[9] By making "jealousy" an abstraction, Pound lessens the dramatic conflict and minimizes the tension between the Christian and secular values noted above.

Pound was not content with the language of this version, and he dropped the poem from subsequent editions of his work, until he retranslated it in "Homage à la Langue d'Oc." However, neither of these albas is merely an exercise in translation; they illustrate Pound's fascination with this *genre* and his insistence upon its central position in Provençal culture.

Another translation that not only defines certain aspects of the culture but that also functions as a persona is "From Syria: The Song of Peire Bremon 'Lo Tort' that he made for his Lady in Provença: he being in Syria a crusader," first published in *Personae* (1909). Little is known of Peire Bremon; this is apparently his only extant work. His *vida* states simply: "Peire Bremon lo Tort [the twisted one] was a poor knight from Vianes.

[8] The influence of the Pre-Raphaelites and the *fin-de-siècle* poets on Pound is discussed in Jackson, *The Early Poetry of Ezra Pound*, pp. 17-47, 119-185.

[9] James J. Wilhelm, *The Cruelest Month: Spring, Nature and Love in Classical and Medieval Lyrics* (New Haven, 1965), p. 197.

16

And he composed well, and was honored by all good men."[10] In *The Spirit of Romance*, Pound rated this poem the equal of Bernart de Ventadorn's "Quant ieu vey la lauzeta mover" and Peire Vidal's "Ab l'alen tir vas me l'aire," two poems that he considers among "the finest songs of Provence" (*SR*, 48). Few critics or editors share Pound's enthusiasm. In a note following the poem he calls it "the only bit of Peire Bremon's work that has come down to us and through its being printed with the songs of Giraut of Bornelh he is like to lose credit for even this."[11] Pound presents this translation with the zeal of a graduate student making an "original" discovery (he was twenty-five at the time). Yet, although he surely overvalued this poem (he dropped it from all further editions of his work), it is thematically important with regard to his other work of this period, for it depicts the poet in exile, addressing his loved one from across the sea, a variation on the *amor de lonh* theme so common in Provençal poetry. His use of Bremon as a persona here is quite effective. Through him Pound "enter[s] an unfamiliar world, develop[s] . . . the thoughts and feelings indigenous to that world, and articulate[s] them in English."[12] Behind Pound's distinctive voice we hear the echo of Peire Bremon. This voice is also the voice of "In Durance," the voice of the poet who wrote from Europe, "This book is for Mary Moore of Trenton, if she wants it." Thus "From Syria," like Pound's other translations,

[10] Jean Boutière and A. H. Schutz, eds., *Biographies des Troubadours* (Paris, 1964), p. 497. Translation mine.

[11] This is not accurate, for it was in print at that time under the name of Peire Bremon lo Tort, in Appel, *Provenzalische Chrestomathie*, pp. 62-63, a volume that Pound owned.

[12] Hugh Kenner, Introduction to *The Translations of Ezra Pound* (New York, 1953), p. 11.

17

has a thematic relevance to his total *oeuvre* that should
not be overlooked:

> In April when I see all through
> Mead and garden new flowers blow,
> And streams with ice-bands broken flow,
> Eke hear the birds their singing do;
> When spring's grass-perfume floateth by
> Then 'tis sweet song and birdlet's cry
> Do make mine old joy come anew.
>
> Such time was wont my thought of old
> To wander in the ways of love.
> Burnishing arms and clang thereof,
> And honour-services manifold
> Be now my need. Whoso combine
> Such works, love is his bread and wine,
> Wherefore should his fight the more be bold.
>
> Song bear I, who tears should bring
> Sith ire of love mak'th me annoy,
> With song think I to make me joy.
> Yet ne'er have I heard said this thing:
> "He sings who sorrow's guise should wear."
> Natheless I will not despair
> That sometime I'll have cause to sing.
>
> I should not to despair give way
> That somewhile I'll my lady see.
> I trust well He that lowered me
> Hath power again to make me gay.
> But if e'er I come to my Love's land
> And turn again to Syrian strand,
> God keep me there for a fool, alway!
>
> God for a miracle well should
> Hold my coming from her away,
> And hold me in His grace alway

18

That I left her, for holy-rood.
An I lose her, no joy for me.
Pardi, hath the wide world in fee.
Nor could he mend it, if He would.

Well did she know sweet wiles to take
My heart, when thence I took my way.
'Thout sighing, pass I ne'er a day
For that sweet semblance she did make
To me, saying all in sorrow:
"Sweet friend, and what of me to-morrow?"
"Love mine, why wilt me so forsake?"

Envoi

Beyond sea be thou sped, my song,
And, by God, to my Lady say
That in desirous, grief-filled way
My nights and my days are full long.
And command thou William the Long-Seer
To tell thee to my Lady dear,
That comfort be her thoughts among.

Here Pound has retained the rhyme scheme of the Provençal stanza (although there the same rhymes are repeated in each stanza), as well as a close approximation of the metrical scheme. The diction is one with which we are by now familiar: archaisms such as "Natheless," "sith," "Pardi," and Pre-Raphaelite medievalisms such as "mead," "holy-rood," and "guise" abound, and Pound's compound creations ("grass-perfume" and "honour-services") contribute to this tone. The problem both here and in the other translations discussed is that Pound has not yet created an equivalent language for the Provençal, but rather is simply accepting the "poetic language" of his day: he is pouring old wine in old bottles, and the results are not very satisfactory. What he later said of his translations of Guido Cavalcanti is equally true here: "What obfuscated me was not the Italian but the crust of dead English, the sediment present in my own available vocabulary. . . . I hadn't in 1910 made a language, I don't mean a language to use, but even a language to think in" (*LE*, 193-194: 1910-1934).

Pound has, however, made several interesting transformations of his text, which prefigure the more inventive textual changes of his later translations. The changes in the second stanza are characteristic. The Provençal reads:

> En cest temps soli' yeu pensar
> cossi·m pogues d'amor iauzir:
> ab cavalgar et ab garnir
> et ab servir et ab onrar;
>> qui aquestz mestiers auria,
>> per els es amors iauzia
> e deu la·n hom mielhs conquistar.[13]

> [At this time I was accustomed to think
> Of how I could delight in love:
> To go on horseback and to dress well;
> And to serve and to honor;
>> Whoever would have that profession,
>> For them is love playing
> And she must be well conquered.]

Pound's first two lines are imprecise, and lack the force of the Provençal. "My thought of old" is vague and "to wander" has no feeling for the *joi d'amor* implicit in the Provençal ("d'amor iauzir"). In the original, the poet is considering what can be gained from love: Pound's per-

[13] Text in Appel, *Provenzalische Chrestomathie*, pp. 62-63.

sona is simply pondering the "ways of love." The third
line has been transformed to some advantage: Pound's
vivid image conjures up a vision of a medieval knight on
horseback, and includes the sense of both "cavalgar" and
"garnir." In the last two lines Pound elaborates upon the
Provençal, with an image that is totally absent from the
Provençal text, and yet that closely resembles the imagery
of the troubadours: "love is his bread and wine." It quali-
fies his love from both a religious and secular viewpoint,
and is characteristic of the type of expansion Pound was
to develop to perfection.

Another translation from this period that serves as a
persona is Pound's version of Bertran de Born's *planh*,
"Si tuit li dol elh plor elh marrimen" (1909). Moreover,
it is the only translation from this period that Pound has
preserved in his *Personae* of 1926. The *planh* ("funeral
lament," from Latin *planctus*) is one of two poems by
Bertran commemorating the death of Henry II's eldest
son, Henry, the "young English King." Bertran greatly
admired the "young English King" and persuaded him to
join with him against Richard Coeur-de-Lion. Richard
had earlier sided with Bertran's brother, Constantin, in
his attempt to retain "Altafort," Bertran's castle. Bertran
did not forget this, and he formed a league against Rich-
ard, who was then Duke of Aquitaine. Henry II mo-
mentarily reconciled his sons, but young Henry later
revolted against his father and, with Bertran, attacked
Richard. Before the campaign could be completed he
fell ill, and on June 11, 1183 he died of the fever at
Martel.[14]

---

[14] The historical background is presented in some detail in
Thomas E. Connolly, "Ezra Pound's 'Near Perigord': The
Background of a Poem," *Comparative Literature*, VIII (Spring
1956), pp. 110-121; Chaytor, *The Troubadours of Dante*, pp.

Bertran's *planh* is written in five eight-line stanzas of decasyllabic verse, with a rhyme scheme of AbabCddE. The repetition of the first and last words of each stanza ("marrimen" and "ira") creates a ground bass which underscores the mournful tone of lament. A preponderance of long vowel sounds (especially ō and ī) also contributes to this tone.

Similar rhyme schemes (and particularly the repetition of one word from stanza to stanza, as in the sestina) were popular in Provençal poetry and here the repetition is quite effective. Bertran also utilizes repetition within a stanza to develop his theme. A good example of this is the word play on "dol" ("sadness") and its variations ("dolors," "dolen," and "doloros") in the first stanza. The repetition of the word "mon" ("world") in each stanza emphasizes the feeling of loss on the part of those who must remain in this world without the presence of "lo jove rei engles."

Throughout the poem Henry is depicted as possessing a catalogue of courtly virtues: "Pretz" and "Jovens" (translated by Pound as "Worth" and "Youth") mourn his passing; he is, in Pound's translation, "fine and amorous," "most valiant," and one who "made the freest hand seem covetous." Thus Henry is portrayed as a platonic ideal, a person embodying all the finest qualities associated with the life of the court. Bertran (and Pound, through the persona of Bertran) is therefore aligning himself with an "ideal"; viewed in this context, he becomes a person of more complexity than simply a lover of "strife."

133-134; and James J. Wilhelm, *Seven Troubadours: The Creators of Modern Verse* (University Park and London, 1970), pp. 145-172.

Pound maintains the original order of the stanzas, with its three-part structure characteristic of this *genre*: the expression of the poet's grief, the elegy for the departed, and the invocation to God to look after the soul of the departed. He drops the strict rhyme scheme of the original, although he retains the repetition of the last words of the first, fifth, and eighth lines (translated as "bitterness," "the young English King," and "ire and sadness" in stanzas I-III and simply as "sadness" in the last two stanzas). Much of the internal repetition is preserved as well: thus, in stanza 1, we find "grief" and "grieving," "ever" and "every," and "dolour" and "dolorous." Pound also creates a pattern of long vowel sounds so that the tonal effect of his translation is similar to the original. His archaisms catch the sense and feeling of the Provençal well, as in "liegemen" (l. 10) for "soudadier" ("one who works for a wage"), and "dolour" for "dolors" ("sadness").[15] A more significant change occurs in the last stanza (l. 35), where Pound translates "E receup mort a nostre salvamen" ("And received death for our salvation") as "Who drank of death for our salvacioun," thus creating an image far more vivid than anything in the Provençal. Pound's misreading of line 12, however, blurs the meaning of the poem. The Provençal ("Trop an agut en Mort mortal guerrier") means: "They [i.e., the troubadours and the jongleurs] have found in Death a deadly warrior." Apparently Pound read "en" as "Sir" (*domine>en*) rather than as the preposition "en" ("in"); the resulting translation ("O'er much hath ta'en Sir Death

---

[15] Pound mentions the problem of diction in his discussion of Daniel in *The Spirit of Romance* (p. 26): "Very often a Romance or Latin word stands between two English words, or includes them." One can see here Pound's first tentative attempts to create a language that is the equivalent of Provençal.

23

that deadly warrior") confuses the sense of the line.

In general, Pound's poem is more pessimistic than Bertran's; this is emphasized by his translation of "marrimen" ("wretchedness") as "bitterness" and "ira" ("gloominess" or "anger") as "ire." This tendency is clear in lines 25-26: the Provençal reads "If love flees from this weak world, full of sadness, I hold his joy to be untrue," which Pound translates as "From this faint world, how full of bitterness/ Love takes his way and holds his joy deceitful." For Bertran there exists a possibility that love may not be leaving this world: in Pound's version this possibility is negated. There is a great feeling of loss in both poems, but the bitterness resulting from this loss is stronger in Pound's version than in the original.

Pound's translation of this poem is uniquely successful among these early efforts, because he creates a sense of movement and a uniformity of tone that convey the gravity of the original. In order to measure Pound's achievement, one need only compare it with the earlier English translations of this poem by Francis Hueffer (1878) and Ida Farnell (1896). All three of these translations are quite literal, and generally draw upon the same poetic diction, yet Pound's translation achieves a fluidity of movement not found in the others. Compare, for example, the opening lines of each version:[16]

> Si tuit li dol elh plor elh marrimen
> E las dolors elh dan elh chaitivier
> Qu'om anc auzis en est segle dolen

[16] Provençal text in Antoine Thomas, *Poésies Complètes de Bertran de Born* (Toulouse, 1888), p. 28; Francis Hueffer, *The Troubadours: A History of Provençal Life and Literature in The Middle Ages* (London, 1878), p. 201; Ida Farnell, *The Lives of the Troubadours* (London, 1896), pp. 110-111.

Fosson ensems, sembleran tuit leugier
Contra la mort del jove rei engles . . .

Hueffer   If all the pain, the grief, the bitter tears,
The sorrow, the remorse, the scornful slight,
Of which man in this life the burden bears
Were thrown a-heap, their balance would be light
Against the death of our young English King . . .

Farnell   If all the pain, and misery, and woe,
The tears, the losses with misfortune fraught,
That in this dark life man can ever know,
Were heap'd together—all would seem as naught
Against the death of the young English king . . .

Pound   If all the grief and woe and bitterness,
All dolour, ill and every evil chance
That ever came upon this grieving world
Were set together they would seem but light
Against the death of the young English King . . .

(P, 36)

Hueffer's version is extremely awkward: the inert articles create a broken, choppy rhythm and the natural order of the Provençal is sacrificed in line 3 in order to maintain the rhyme scheme. His diction is a compilation of Victorian clichés. But most important, Hueffer's version lacks any development: the terms of grief are literally "thrown a-heap" and they remain just that.

Farnell's version suffers from some of the same problems—the broken rhythm of the first two lines, the unnatural order of lines 2 and 3 (forced upon her by the rhyme scheme), and the awkward translation of the first half of line 4. Like Hueffer's translation, Farnell's remains a mere accumulation of terms "heap'd together" but lacking organic unity.

Pound clearly overcomes the faults of his predecessors. His diction is more precise, and, as we have seen, he maintains the internal repetition of the original. In his version there is an accretion of terms, building to a climax in line 4. He achieves this by his choice of words, his elimination of unnecessary articles, and his enjambment in lines 2 and 3. As a result, Pound's rendition not only has the surface fidelity of the other versions, but it also maintains a fidelity to the rhythm of the poet's speech, and it is this which distinguishes his translation.

These translations from *Personae* and *Exultations* show Pound beginning to develop his notion of what a translation is and how it relates to the original. None of these translations is strictly literal—in even the most literal he transforms the text in a way to make it characteristically his own. The search for a language is Pound's principal problem: his diction suffers from the strong influence of Rossetti, Morris, and the poets of the nineties. Although traces of this language recur in his next major group of translations, Pound has begun to liberate himself from his immediate poetic inheritance.

The Spirit of Romance (1910) contains stanzas (some in verse, some in prose) from over forty Provençal poems, representing the work of seventeen poets.[17] However, with the exception of the chapter on Daniel, Pound's presentation is rather haphazard. "Proença" (Chapter III) is the outcome of an enormous amount of reading and scholarship, and yet it suffers from having been written

[17] These poets are Arnaut Daniel, Bernart de Ventadorn, Jaufre Rudel, Bertran de Born, Peire Vidal, Giraut de Bornelh, Aimeric de Belenoi, Aimeric de Pegulhan, Folquet de Marselha, Arnaut de Mareuil, Sordello, Guilhem d'Autpol, Peire de Corbiac, Lo Monge de Montaudon, Peire Cardenal, Marcabrun, and Giraut Riquier.

as the framework for a series of lecture notes. From 1908-1910 Pound was teaching part time at The Polytechnic, and one of his early lectures was on "The Rise of Song in Provence. The Troubadours."[18] Indeed, the material covered in that lecture could almost be a table of contents for Chapters II and III of *The Spirit of Romance*: "The Belangal Alba, Bernard of Ventadorn, Bertrand of Born, Giraut of Borneilh, Jaufre Rudel, Arnaut Daniel, Pere Bremon Lo Tort, Peire Cardinal, Sordello and King Richard Coeur de Lion."[19] Perhaps eighty percent of the material in "Proença" consists of translations; although there is some discussion of the poets, there is very little commentary on the poems themselves. The selection, however, is in itself significant, as Pound makes clear in the introduction: "My criticism has consisted in selection rather than in presentation of opinion" (*SR*, 9). This is the method of "Luminous Detail,"[20] by which one can define a culture through representative excerpts—a method refined upon in his *ABC of Reading* and *The Cantos*. By judicious quotation, Pound attempts here to isolate and communicate the outstanding qualities of each troubadour's verse that, taken together, define the culture as a whole.

For the most part these translations are quite literal; even when the translation is in verse, Pound strives less for "poetic effects" than in his earlier translations. The language is more natural, with a preference for the "unperturbed order, almost . . . of prose" (*SR*, 38) that he noticed in the poetry of Daniel. In this respect, these translations are an important exercise for Pound: not only

[18] Quoted in Norman, *Ezra Pound*, p. 31.
[19] *Ibid.*, pp. 31-32.
[20] Ezra Pound, "I Gather the Limbs of Osiris, II" *New Age*, x, 6 (7 Dec. 1911), p. 130. Hereafter called "Osiris."

is he exposed to a great number of Provençal poets and forced to select critically from among their works, thus refining his own definition of the essentials of Provençal culture, but technically he is able to divest himself of much of the archaic diction that had earlier plagued him. He is able, at least to some extent, to begin to "purify the language of the tribe" and thus to forge a poetic language of his own.

Before proceeding further, we should examine a characteristic translation from this work. The two stanzas of Peire Vidal's "Ab l'alen tir vas me l'aire" that Pound has translated into verse will serve quite well:

> Ab l'alen tir vas me l'aire
> qu'eu sen venir de Proensa:
> tot quant es de lai m'agensa,
> si que, quan n'aug ben retraire,
> eu m'o escout en rizen
> en deman per un mot cen:
> tan m'es bel quan n'aug ben dire.
>
> Qu'om no sap tan dous repaire
> cum de Rozer tro qu'a Vensa,
> si cum clau mars e Durensa,
> ni on tan fis jois s'esclaire.
> per qu'entre la franca gen
> ai laissat mon cor jauzen
> ab leis que fals iratz rire.[21]
>
> Breathing I draw the air to me
> Which I feel coming from Provença,
> All that is thence so pleasureth me

[21] Text in Karl Bartsch, *Peire Vidal's Lieder* (Berlin, 1857), p. 35. Francis Hueffer has also translated this poem (*The Troubadours*, p. 175).

That whenever I hear good speech of it
I listen laughing and straightway
Demand for each word an hundred
So fair to me is the hearing.

No man hath known such sweet repair
'Twixt Rhone and the Vensa.
Or from the shut sea to Durensa,
Nor any place with such joys
As there are among the French folk where
I left my heart a-laughing in her care,
Who turns the veriest sullen unto laughter.

(*SR*, 49)

Although Pound has called all the translations in this work "merely exegetic," the two stanzas given here are more than simply a line-by-line translation of the original. To begin with, Pound has tried to preserve a line length resembling the Provençal and in the second stanza he has retained a good deal of rhyme as well. In order to maintain a uniform line length, Pound has dropped phrases from the Provençal and added English phrases where none exist in the original. For example, in line 5 of the first stanza he has added "and straightway," and from line 6 of the same stanza he has dropped "ben dire." Nor does he hesitate to follow the lead of the Provençal and adopt words in English not usually used in this sense, such as "repair" (l. 8) and "demand" (l. 6), as he had done earlier in his translation of Bertran's *planh*. There remain some traces of the diction of his earlier poems, such as "pleasureth," but the language is generally modern.

The second stanza suffers, however, from a mistranslation that confuses the meaning of the original. In

29

Pound's version there appears to be a contrast between Provence and Northern France ("among the French folk") that does not exist in the original. The Provençal has a logic that Pound's translation lacks:

> [For no man knows such a sweet resting place
> As the area from the Rhone to Vence,
> Which the sea and the Durance enclose
> Nor any place where such a pure joy illuminates
>   everything.
> That's why, among these noble people,
> I have left my happy heart
> With her who makes the angry one laugh.]

It is also surprising that Pound eliminates the notion of the illumination of the beloved. However, it is not our purpose to dwell on his errors, but rather to show how he orders a "literal" translation. Here too he has condensed and expanded to maintain a uniformity of line length. He has also made an effort to create a translation that is easily readable, and he has certainly succeeded in doing that.

Throughout these translations Pound achieves a greater freedom in terms of diction than was the case in the earlier translations. Although still without an English equivalent for the Provençal, he seems to be gradually getting away from his earlier use of stock phrases and archaisms. Moreover even here, in what he calls "exegetic" translations, considerable liberties are taken with the text, and the resulting translations are much more than mere paraphrases. What is most lacking in his chapter in *The Spirit of Romance* is the sort of systematic interpretation of Provençal poetry that he presents in the quasi-historic essay "Troubadours: Their Sorts and Conditions" (1913), or the mystic approach of "Psychology and Troubadours" (1912). It was no doubt to fill this gap that Pound later added the latter essay to his book.

Another series of translations that helped Pound in his development as a poet was published by Walter Morse Rummel under the *fin-de-siècle* title of *Hesternae Rosae* (Roses of Yesterday), 1913. Rummel's work was an edition of nine twelfth- and thirteenth-century troubadour songs with piano accompaniment and French and English translations. Pound assisted in the choice of poems and prepared the English versions. In the "Preface," Rummel credits Pound ("an ardent proclaimer of the artistic side of mediaeval poetry")[22] with helping to give the melodies the proper rhythm and ligature. Obviously, Pound's purpose in such an endeavor is vastly different from that of his earlier translations or even his versions in *The Spirit of Romance.* Most important, of course, is the fact that these versions are meant to be sung, not spoken or read. All of the songs are chosen for their melodies: apart from the two songs by Arnaut Daniel, the one by Bernart de Ventadorn, and the anonymous ballad "A l'entra del tens clar," the songs are rather obscure, and have texts that are not noteworthy. Although Pound's translations of these nine poems are not outstanding, they do form an important stage in his development as a translator.

The quality of these translations is easily observable. Bernart de Ventadorn's "Quant l'herba fresq el fuell apar"[23] is characteristic of them:

> When grass starts green and flowers rise
> A leaf in garden and inclose

[22] Walter Morse Rummel, *Hesternae Rosae* (London and Boston, 1913), p. v.
[23] Text in Appel, *Provenzalische Chrestomathie*, pp. 58-59.

31

And philomel in dulcet cries
And lifted notes his heart bestows.
Joy I've in him and in the flowers joy
E'en joy in me have I yet more employ
Hath joy in her in whom my joy is cast
She is such joy as hath all joys o'er past.

I love her so and so her prize
I fear her and such thoughts oppose
That my poor words dare not arise,
Nor speech nor deeds my heart disclose.
And yet she knows the depth of my annoy
And, when she will, she will her grace employ
For God's love, Love, put now our love to test
For time goes by and we here waste his best.

Pound has made a number of textual transformations here, but all of them are subordinated to his desire to reproduce the rhyme scheme and musicality of the original. He is not too successful, for, in order to achieve his effect, he is forced to make some unusual inversions and to add words simply for padding. This poem, however, should be judged for what it is—a song in which the prime concern is the musicality of the verse. Because Pound's emphasis in these poems is different from his earlier work, his development as a result of these exercises is also quite different. His language is certainly more modern, and his verse achieves a greater flexibility and naturalness.

Between *Hesternae Rosae* and "Homage à la Langue d'Oc" (1918), Pound continued to work on his translations of Arnaut Daniel that had begun appearing in *The New Age* at the end of 1911 and that he planned to have published in one volume. Apart from this group of poems, however, only one further translation from Provençal appeared during this period: his version of Bertran de Born's "Dompna pois de me no'us cal." Although it was not published until 1914, Pound had translated part of it as early as 1908, and was aware of its significance even earlier than this. For Bertran's attempt to create a "borrowed lady" to replace the woman whose favour he has lost is a metaphor for the poetic activity of both Bertran and Pound: not only is the poet's goal the creation of an ideal beauty, but this beauty is composed of diverse elements taken from many sources. Bertran's method here is analogous to Pound's use of material in poems like "Na Audiart," "Near Perigord," and especially *The Cantos*. Pound's estimation of the importance of this poem can be seen by the fact that it is the only Provençal translation—apart from Bertran's *planh*—that he includes in his *Personae* of 1926.

Pound's translation of "Dompna Pois" is certainly more inventive than his translation of the *planh*, but ultimately it succeeds less. To begin with, it presents more formal difficulties. Like the *planh*, the rhyme scheme and line pattern are identical in each stanza, although this pattern does not involve the repetition of the same word from stanza to stanza. Each of the seven stanzas has ten lines and follows a strict pattern, although these lines vary in length from four to eight syllables. The rhyme scheme is abbcddeeff, and thus the couplets require from fourteen to sixteen words with the same rhyme. Pound has avoided this problem by retaining only the final couplet and leaving most of the remaining lines unrhymed. He has also dropped the strict pattern of line length. Certainly Pound has the option of altering the formal aspects of the original, but here he seems unable to provide an alternative way of ordering the poem. In the original there is a tension between the strict form and the movement of the lines that propels the poem forward, but Pound's version lacks this tension. In spite of these formal weaknesses, the poem is interesting for what it suggests about Pound's principles of translation.

One notices a change in diction from the earlier translation of Bertran, and indeed all the translations prior to *The Spirit of Romance* and *Hesternae Rosae*. There the poems at times seemed overwhelmed by the archaisms. Here a few archaic forms persist (chiefly the verbs), but the language is surprisingly modern in comparison. Like the translations in *The Spirit of Romance*, Pound shows a preference here for a natural subject-verb-object order, and for the active voice. He is also much more free in his changes: individual words and whole lines are dropped and added and new images and metaphors are formed. There are minor deletions (such as Bels Cembelins' "fresca color natural," which simply becomes "color"), and more important deletions, such as the dropping of the envoy. Indeed, the translation is highly interpretative, as a close study of several stanzas will indicate. The alterations of the third stanza are representative of the poem as a whole: [24]

> Fresca color natural
> pren, bels Cembelins, de vos
> el doutz esgart amoros
> e fatz gran sobrieira,
> car rei lais,
> c'anc res de ben nous sofrais;
> mi donz na Elis deman
> son adreich parlar gaban,

[24] Text in *Bertran de Born, Sein Leben und Seine Werke*, ed. Albert Stimming (Halle, 1879), pp. 148-150. Farnell has also translated this poem (*The Lives of the Troubadours*, pp. 114-117).

quem don a mi donz ajuda,
pois non er fada ni muda.

Bels Cembelins, I take of you your colour,
For it's your own, and your glance
Where love is,
A proud thing I do here,
For, as to colour and eyes
I shall have missed nothing at all,
Having yours.
I ask of Midons Aelis (of Montfort)
Her straight speech free-running,
That my phantom lack not in cunning.

(P, 105)

We see at once that although both stanzas have ten lines, considerable additions and deletions have been made. The two adjectives describing her color have been dropped, and "de vos" has become "For it's your own," which is certainly more vivid than the Provençal. The same effect is achieved in the following line where "el doutz esgart amoros" ("your sweet amorous glance") becomes "your glance/ Where love is." The next two lines of Provençal have been expanded into three lines in the English version. Pound has added "as to color and eyes" to clarify the Provençal, where, as we have seen, there is a specific mention of color, but no mention of eyes. He also adds a place name for identification, since it is important to him that each lady be associated with a different castle, as his interpretation of this poem in "Near Perigord" demonstrates. Her "adreich parlar gaban" ("Witty ingenious discourse") becomes "straight speech free-running," another interpretation that enlivens the text. In order to maintain the uniformity of a ten-line stanza, Pound condenses the last two lines of the Provençal into one.

Here we see a type of transformation that will become characteristic of Pound and that illustrates one of his favorite principles: "Dichten = condensare" (*ABC*, 36). The Provençal reads: "That she (Elis) give aid to my lady/ since now she (i.e., his "borrowed" lady) neither enchants nor is distinctive," which becomes "That my phantom lack not in cunning." Pound's "phantom" (suggested, no doubt, by "fadar," "to enchant") is a far more elusive and mysterious figure than the "borrowed lady" of the Provençal. She is not a mere compilation of the characteristics of others, but possesses an ethereal quality quite lacking in Bertran's poem. The fact that the "borrowed lady" becomes a "phantom" for Pound precludes the possibility of physical contact—which is obviously an important element in the Bertran-Maent relationship. Here, rather, the "phantom" is what Hugh Witemeyer calls in another context "that essential beauty [which] has its earthly incarnation in a variety of individual (in this case, female) forms."[25] In *The Spirit of Romance* Pound speaks of "the splendors of paradise" in a way that is not unrelated to his "phantom" here:

"They are ineffable and innumerable and no man having beheld them can fittingly narrate them or even remember them exactly. Nevertheless by naming over all the most beautiful things we know we may draw back upon the mind some vestige of the heavenly splendor.

"I suggest that the troubadour, either more indolent or more logical, progresses from correlating all these details for purposes of comparison, and lumps the matter. The lady contains the catalogue, is more complete. She serves as sort of *mantram*" (*SR*, 96-97).

[25] Hugh Witemeyer, *The Poetry of Ezra Pound: Forms and Renewal, 1908-1920* (Berkeley and Los Angeles, 1969), p. 13.

Pound develops this concept further in "Na Audiart," as we shall see later.

The final stanza defines the nature of this "phantom" in greater detail, by contrasting her with Maent:

> Belz Senher, eu nous quier al
> mas que fos tant cobeitos
> d'aquesta cum sui de vos,
> c'una lechadieira
> amors nais,
> don mos cors es tant lechais,
> mais vuolh de vos lo deman
> que autra tener baisan;
> doncs mi donz per quem refuda,
> pois sap que tant l'ai volguda?

> Ah, Bels Senher, Maent, at last
> I ask naught from you,
> Save that I have such a hunger for
> This phantom
> As I've for you, such flame-lap,
> And yet I'd rather
> Ask of you than hold another,
> Mayhap, right close and kissed,
> Ah, Lady, why have you cast
> Me out, knowing you hold me fast!
>
> (P, 106-107)

Again we find expansion for the sake of clarification: "Bels Senher" ("handsome Lord") is purposely obscure in Provençal, for the function of the *senhal* is to conceal the identity of the person being addressed. Pound identifies his lady as Maent, and the line that follows is a direct translation of the first line of the Provençal. Pound then transforms the Provençal in an interesting way. Trans-

37

lated literally, the next two lines read: "Except that I be so greedy/ for that (i.e., his "borrowed lady"), as I am for you/ Let a passionate/ love be born/ for which my body is so lustful." Pound translates "cobeitos" as hunger, and then condenses lines 4-6 of the Provençal into the single image of "flame-lap," which qualifies the nature of his desire in a special way. Bertran would like to have a lustful ("lechais") relationship with his lady, but the nature of the "phantom" precludes the possibility of "flame-lap." In contrast to his passion for Maent, which is physical, de Born's relationship to this "phantom," in Pound's version, can never be anything but spiritual and other-worldly. Thus Pound shies away from the blatant sexuality of the Provençal, preferring instead a more ethereal relationship. This alteration is important in terms of Pound's developing love ethic.

Pound's translation of the final couplet is another example of his vivification of the Provençal. In the original, the poet refers to his lady in the third person: "Then my lady, why does she refuse me, since she knows how much I wanted her?" Pound's version has a poignancy and an immediacy lacking in the Provençal:

> Ah, lady, why have you cast
> Me out, knowing you hold me so fast!

These two stanzas indicate, then, the different types of changes Pound makes in the original. Although he is not able to find a suitable form for this translation, the transformations he makes in it are far more interesting than those in the *planh*. The use of a persona is more sophisticated here, for the poem has a greater thematic relevance for Pound than the *planh*. Pound's "phantom" becomes a platonic ideal, the female counterpart of the "young English King." Moreover, the poem is a metaphor for the poet's activity, as he assembles "Luminous Details" into a coherent whole. This was a method Pound would follow with great success.

Throughout these early translations Pound slowly alters his concept of a translation as he develops technically as a poet. His language becomes increasingly free of the poetic diction of the nineties, and his versions become more and more interpretative. Apart from their value as technical exercises, many of these poems function as personae, and thus have an important thematic role in Pound's total *oeuvre*. T. S. Eliot, discussing some of Pound's other early translations, put the matter well: ". . . good translation like this is not merely translation, for the translator is giving the original through himself, and finding himself through the original."[26]

[26] Introduction to *Ezra Pound: Selected Poems*, ed. T. S. Eliot (London, 1928), p. 13.

Chapter II

RESUSCITATION OF THE PAST:
The Provençal Personae

> If one can really penetrate the life of another age,
> one is penetrating the life of one's own.
> > T. S. Eliot, Introduction to
> > *Ezra Pound: Selected Poems*

> I have walked over these roads;
> I have thought of them living.
> > "Provincia Deserta"

AMONG Pound's early experiments with Provençal poetry, only the studies of individual poets—"Marvoil," "Piere Vidal Old," "Sestina: Altaforte," "Na Audiart," and "Near Perigord"—and the two translations of Bertran de Born discussed earlier remain in the 1926 edition of *Personae*. As examples of either personae or "criticism in a new composition" (*LE*, 75:1934), these poems have an obvious importance in Pound's *oeuvre* that has not gone unnoticed.[1] But more than this, they constitute Pound's first poetic interpretation of Provençal culture, revealing those aspects of the culture which became an important part of his *Weltanschauung*, as well as prefiguring many of the themes and techniques of *The Cantos*. For this reason they can best be considered as a group.

[1] See, for example, N. Christoph de Nagy, *The Poetry of Ezra Pound: The Pre-Imagist Stage* (Bern, 1968); Witemeyer, *The Poetry of Ezra Pound*; and Jackson, *The Early Poetry of Ezra Pound*.

Pound presents a wide selection of troubadour poets in *The Spirit of Romance*. One is justified in asking why he singles out Peire Vidal, Arnaut de Mareuil, and Bertran de Born for particular attention as personae.[2] What, besides the fact that they were all contemporaries, writing at the end of the twelfth century, do they have in common? Their significance is not apparent in *The Spirit of Romance*, where only one poem by Vidal and Mareuil is cited, and where Bertran de Born is praised for qualities other than his skill as a poet. If, as Witemeyer has stated, Pound's personae "combine his concern for revitalizing history with his concern for portraying dramatic ecstasy ... [and] are exercises in historical imagination and also in creating a vivid personal identity,"[3] any number of Provençal poets might have fulfilled these requirements. After all, for Pound the "culture of Provence finds perhaps its finest expression in the works of Arnaut Daniel" (*SR*, 39); yet, although he was to translate many of Daniel's works, no poem of Pound's utilizes Daniel as subject matter.

In his chapter on Villon in *The Spirit of Romance*, Pound clarifies his interest in these poets: "Villon's verse is real, because he lived it; as Bertran de Born, as Arnaut Marvoil, as that mad poseur Vidal, he lived it. For these men life is in the press. No brew of books, no distillation of sources will match the tang of them" (*SR*, 178). The author of a Provençal *vida*, writing as much as a century after the death of the poet, had very little material from which to construct his biography, apart from the poet's works. Moreover, his sole purpose was to present an entertaining biography, so that his listeners would be in-

[2] Pound uses the Anglicized version of Mareuil (Marvoil), and often misspells Peire (Piere).

[3] Witemeyer, *The Poetry of Ezra Pound*, p. 60.

41

terested in the songs that followed. He often assumed that the material in the poems was autobiographical, and thus in a certain sense many Provençal poets were made to "live" their verse in their *vidas*. This is clearly the case with Vidal: the author of his *vida* was a very literal reader of his poetry; consequently he made Vidal's life correspond to the extravagant metaphors and similes of his work. Pound, too, chooses to emphasize this aspect of Vidal's character. Other poets, like Bertran de Born, certainly did live their poetry, and, as we have seen, Pound stresses this by considering "Dompna Pois" as an artifice for "stirring up strife." With Arnaut de Mareuil, however, there is little of the personal extravagance that marks the lives of Vidal and Bertran. According to his *vida*, Arnaut sang of only one lady; although this fact is important for Pound, his interpretation of Arnaut's life is entirely his own. Like the composers of the *vidas* (and Pound often prefaces his works with pseudo-*vidas*) Pound interprets, expands, and rearranges his materials so that his recreation of the poet's life and works becomes a blend of "fact" and "fiction." In almost every case the result is a poem that attempts to interpret the "real" character of the poet being presented, rather than relying solely upon the image presented by his poems. Moreover, each poet represents for Pound a special aspect of Provençal culture: Bertran is the man of action, whose poems have the power to move kingdoms; Arnaut shows the absolute devotion of a troubadour to his lady; and Vidal is an example of the close connection between man and the vital universe, as revealed (or symbolized) by his metamorphosis.

In a now famous letter to William Carlos Williams, Pound defined the focus of these poems: "To me the short so-called dramatic lyric—at any rate the sort of thing I do—is the poetic part of a drama the rest of which (to me the prose part) is left to the reader's imagination or implied or set in a short note. I catch the character I happen to be interested in at the moment he interests me, usually a moment of song, self-analysis, or sudden understanding or revelation. . . . I paint my man as I *conceive* him. Et voilà tout!" (*L*, 3-4). What is important here is that Pound is specifying as "poetic" precisely that aspect of Vidal's, Arnaut's, and Bertran's life and character which is his own invention. His interpretation of these three poets subsumes a *trobar clus* tradition in which the poets "sing not all they have in mind" (*LE*, 101), and in which the reader is constantly being asked to "read between the lines" and "solve the riddle." "Marvoil," "Piere Vidal Old," and "Near Perigord" all provide in one way or another keys to the lives and works of the poets under discussion, and thus are interpretative presentations.

"Marvoil" (1909) is presumably the final poem of Arnaut de Mareuil, the summation and explanation of his life's work (his "will and testament"). It is a very private poem, for Arnaut does not sing it to the world, but rather scribbles it on a piece of parchment and hides it in a wall, where future generations may or may not find it. Mareuil is generally credited with being the inventor of the epistolary *genre* and therefore it is fitting that Pound's poem presents him in the act of composing such a letter. Pound clearly intends "Marvoil" to be the key to Arnaut's other works, for those who find it will "know more of Arnaut of Marvoil / Than half his canzoni say of him."

The poem begins on a note of confession, as Arnaut gives the reasons for his exile, recalls his relationship to his former benefactor (the Vicomte of Beziers), and identifies the Countess of Beziers as his former mistress. The material in these stanzas (1-3) is "factual," drawn

43

principally from the Provençal *vida* and Petrarch's desig-
nation of Arnaut as " 'l men famoso Arnaldo." But
Pound's sources are already interpretative, for both Pe-
trarch and the author of the *vida* wrote long after Ma-
reuil. Nowhere in his poetry does Arnaut reveal the name
of his mistress: only the *vida* gives us this information. As
one editor of his work has stated: "Tout ce qu'on peut
dire, c'est que le poète parle avec une telle sincérité de
sa fidélité à une seule dame . . . qu'il est probable qu'il s'est
servi de plusieurs *senhals*, et qu'il a même évité un *senhal*
dans la plupart de ses poèmes, afin de dérouter les curi-
eux et de cacher à jamais l'identité de celle qu'il aimait."[4]
In fact, Pound has taken exactly the same liberties with
his sources as Petrarch and the author of the *vida* took
with theirs. The "facts" presented in the Provençal *vida*
in no way suggest the character of the poet presented in
these stanzas, nor does the diction of Mareuil's poems re-
semble the Browningesque language employed by Pound.
Like the "seneschal" cursed by Alfonso, Arnaut's total
oeuvre has masked his real feelings: now it is as though
this mask had suddenly been ripped away, revealing a
very passionate person whose rejection has left him filled
with hatred for Alfonso. As Pound later said of his
Homage to Sextus Propertius: "My job was to bring a
dead man to life, to present a living figure" (*L*, 149);
here he has admirably succeeded.

The second half of the poem moves from "life" to
"literature" as Arnaut develops the themes of his "vers
and canzoni" by an extended praise of the Countess. Yet,
since this eulogy is private, it is unlikely that anyone will
ever know of his love for the Countess, and he seems al-
most to desire this. Obviously recognition is not impor-

[4] Introduction to *Les Poésies Lyriques d'Arnaut de Mareuil*,
ed. R. C. Johnson (Paris, 1935), p. xxxi.

tant for Arnaut: what is important is that this love, which has sustained him in the past, will continue to support him even though the object of his love is separated from him. As he contemplates the placement of his poem in the wall, he develops a comparison between this act and his praise of his lady, ending with an image that appears frequently in his verse:[5]

> O hole in the wall here . . .
> Keep yet my secret in thy breast here;
> Even as I keep her image in my heart here.
>
> (*P*, 23)

Taken in its entirety, his "last will and testament" not only recalls the central period of his life (the three years during which he wrote for the Countess) but demonstrates how, in his exile, he continues to derive sustenance from this memory. Thus Arnaut "lives his poetry," by remaining faithful to the themes about which he has sung.

In "Piere Vidal Old" (1909), we have another presentation, through recollection, of a central experience in the life of the poet, one that provides a key to our understanding of both his life and his works. Here too Pound's interpretation of the poet is taken predominately from his *vida*, the essence of which is related in an epigraph to his poem. The author of the *vida* was in turn simply expanding a famous stanza of Vidal's:

> E si tot lop m'appellatz,
> no m'o tenh a dezonor,
> ni sim cridan li pastor
> ni sim sui per lor cassatz:
> et am mais bosc e boisso

[5] Noted in De Nagy, *The Poetry of Ezra Pound*, p. 121.

45

no fauc palaitz ni maizo,
et ab joi li er mos treus
entre vent e gel e neus.[6]

[And although you call me a wolf
I do not hold myself in dishonor,
Not even if the shepherds blame me
Or if I am chased by them;
And I prefer woods and thickets
To palace and home.
And with joy my path will be towards her,
Amid wind and ice and snow.]

As Ernest Hoepffner states: "Prenant cette plaisanterie au
sérieux, et voyant là une preuve éclatante de la folie de
Peire, l'imagination fertile de l'auteur de la *vida* en a fait
une scène réelle et vivante."[7]

Although there can be no question of Vidal's love for
Na Loba (he sings her praise in five songs), the account
given in the *vida* and followed by Pound is surely ficti-
tious. For Pound, Vidal's metamorphosis is symbolic of a
type of transformation he had written of earlier in "The
Tree." Sister M. Bernetta Quinn's discussion of that poem
is relevant here: "Not only does this transformation op-
erate from soul to soul, but also in empathetic fashion be-
tween man and non-human nature. Relationships, truths
otherwise unsuspected, are revealed through entrance
into the life of one's environment."[8]

[6] Text in Bartsch, *Peire Vidal's Lieder*, p. 24.

[7] Ernest Hoepffner, *Le Troubadour Peire Vidal: Sa Vie et
son Oeuvre* (Paris, 1961), p. 88.

[8] Sister M. Bernetta Quinn, "The Metamorphoses of Ezra
Pound," *Motive and Method in The Cantos of Ezra Pound*,
ed. Lewis Leary (New York, 1954), p. 72.

46

Although the account of Vidal's life is a "fiction," Pound utilizes it very effectively for its symbolic value. Pound sees Vidal as an example of man's close relationship to the "vital universe." In "Psychology and Troubadours," Pound clarifies the nature of this relationship:

"Let us consider the body as pure mechanism. Our kinship to the ox we have constantly thrust upon us; but beneath this is our kinship to the vital universe, to the tree and the living rock. . . .

"We have about us the universe of fluid force, and below us the germinal universe of wood alive, of stone alive. Man is—the sensitive physical part of him—a mechanism . . . As to his consciousness, the consciousness of some seems to rest, or to have its center more properly, in what the Greek psychologists called the *phantastikon*. Their minds are, that is, circumvolved about them like soap-bubbles reflecting sundry patches of the macrocosmos. And with certain others their consciousness is 'germinal.' Their thoughts are in them as the thought of the tree is in the seed, or in the grass, or the grain, or the blossom. And these minds are the more poetic, and they affect mind about them, and transmute it as the seed the earth. And this latter sort of mind is close on the vital universe; and the strength of the Greek beauty rests in this, that it is ever at the interpretation of this vital universe, by its signs of gods and godly attendants and oreads" (*SR*, 92-93). Such a mind is Peire Vidal's, who, throughout the poem, is trying to regain contact with this universe.

"Piere Vidal Old" is built on a series of contrasts, principally between the sterility of the present "age gone lax" and the vitality of the "great dead days" when the poet was part of the natural world. Memory redeems Vidal in

47

the present, and permits him to reexperience his past metamorphosis.

The poem begins on a note of recollection, as the vigor of the sun makes the poet aware of the "great dead days" of the past. In the two stanzas that follow, his association with the natural world is developed through his metamorphosis from man to wolf. At first he is only compared to the wolves, but then he is seen as a wolf attacking game and feared by the "grey pack." Pound has chosen the most striking aspect of the wolf's everyday existence to characterize the completeness of Vidal's metamorphosis (notice too that there is no mention of this in the *vida*): his attacking and devouring of game. Significantly it is at just this point that Loba is introduced, and the juxtaposition of her with Vidal's pursuit of the "hind's blood" is indeed striking:

> Hot was that hind's blood yet it scorched me not
> As did first scorn, then lips of the Penautier! (*P*, 30)

The comparable intensity of the two experiences is later reinforced by the parallel structure of the sentences:

> Hot is such love and silent . . .

Here Vidal begins to recreate the one experience that gave his madness meaning, his seduction of Na Loba. This incident too is unsubstantiated in his verse and *vida*. Vidal had, according to his *vida*, stolen a kiss from Na Azalais, the wife of En Barral, with the result that "from fear thereof, [he] entered into a ship and went to Genoa . . . for he was in sore fear lest my Lady Azalais should seek to compass his death."[9] But there is no suggestion

---

[9] Farnell, *The Lives of the Troubadours*, p. 83.

that Vidal had any physical contact with Loba. Others had, however, and her beauty was well known throughout the region. In the *vida* of Raymond of Miraval (also composed by the author of Vidal's *vida*) we read the following:

". . . Now the Loba was exceeding lovely and gracious, and wishful of worth and honour, and all the barons of that region, and all the strangers that looked upon her, loved her—the Count of Foix, Sir Oliver of Saissac, Sir Peire Roger of Mirepoix, Sir Aimeric of Montreal, and Sir Peire Vidal, who made many good songs of her. But Sir Raymond of Miraval loved her more than all, and by song and speech advanced her fame as best he might, even as one who could better do it than any knight alive. Then the Loba, for the great fame he had gotten her in the world, and for the knowledge she had that he could both make or mar her fortunes, suffered his prayers, and pledged to him her love, and bound him to her with a kiss. But in all this she meant but to beguile him, for she loved the Count of Foix so greatly that she had made of him her lover. . . ."[10]

Thus the event is at least in keeping with Loba's character, if not with actual fact. Pound puts the seduction scene in high relief by his use of color adjectives, reminiscent of a similar use by the Pre-Raphaelites. In an early essay on "M. Antonius Flamininus and John Keats," Pound had spoken of "the intense, surcharged beauty of blood and ivory that we find in Rossetti,"[11] and much the same could be said of this poem. The red of the hind's blood and the vividness of the sun contrast with Vidal's

[10] *Ibid.*, p. 181.
[11] Ezra Pound, "M. Antonius Flamininus and John Keats, a Kinship in Genius," *Book News Monthly*, xxvi, 6 (Feb. 1908), p. 466.

present grayness. Vidal was once a part of this vital nat-
ural world, and he longs to regain his power. Loba is
described as a passive "ivorylike" figure, who first appears
(in a beautiful metaphor no doubt suggested by a line
from Daniel),[12] as though propelled by forces greater
then herself. Throughout she is silent, pale, and submis-
sive, and yet she possesses a mockery that makes her Vi-
dal's equal, certainly at the moment of consummation.
Having found his "mate" Vidal finally triumphs:

> Behold here Vidal, that was hunted, flayed,
> Shamed and yet bowed not and that won at last.
>
> (P, 31)

All that remains for him now is a remembrance of that
great event, which he contrasts with the situation around
him:

> O Age gone lax! O stunted followers,
> That mask at passions and desire desires,
> Behold me shrivelled, and your mock of mocks;
> And yet I mock you by the mighty fires
> That burnt me to this ash.   (P, 32)

As Witemeyer correctly points out, this age is both
Pound's and ours, as well as Vidal's, and in the first two
lines "the created mask is mocking its own creator and
all poets who do not live their verse but use personae
instead."[13] This is quite appropriate from another poet
who, Pound felt, "lived his verse," and it is a warning
to others that they should do the same.

Finally, so strong is Vidal's power of recollection, that
he reexperiences his earlier metamorphosis and presum-
ably regains contact with the life-giving force. Vidal has

[12] Noted in Witemeyer, *The Poetry of Ezra Pound*, p. 31.
[13] *Ibid.*, p. 72.

gambled everything and won: yet his success, like Arnaut's, is a private one since, apart from the present work, he shares the memory with no one.

A more public figure is Bertran de Born, whose enigmatic personality fascinated Pound. Pound once wrote to W. C. Williams that Gaudier-Brzeska was "the only person with whom I can really be 'Altaforte'" (*L*, 27), and Charles Norman has pointed out that Pound "identified himself with Bertran de Born quite thoroughly; in . . . 'Near Perigord' . . . he even wonders if the troubadour had 'a red straggling beard' and green eyes, like himself."[14] In addition to the two translations considered in Chapter I, Pound wrote three original poems about him. They are based largely on the two war poems that are partially translated in *The Spirit of Romance* ("Be·m platz lo gais temps de Pascor" and "Un sirventes on motz no falh"), and the two translations discussed above. The first of these original poems, "Na Audiart" (1908), is inspired by the fifth stanza of "Dompna Pois de me No'us cal," a fact Pound makes clear in the prefatory note: "Anyone who has read anything of the troubadours knows well the tale of Bertran of Born and My Lady Maent of Montaignac, and knows also the song he made when she would none of him, the song wherein he, seeking to find or make her equal, begs of each preëminent lady of Langue d'Oc some trait or some fair semblance . . . and even in this fashion of Lady Audiart 'although she would that ill come unto him' he sought and praised the lineaments of the torse. And all this to make 'Una dompna soiseubuda' a borrowed lady or as the Italians translated it 'Una donna ideale'" (*P*, 8).

"Na Audiart" is an extended commentary on the significance of the stanza mentioned above. Through the

[14] Norman, *Ezra Pound*, p. 47.

persona of Bertran de Born, Pound addresses Lady Au-
diart directly, as he had addressed Lady Maent in the
other poem. However, the difference in tone between
these two poems is as great as the difference between Ber-
tran's relationship with the "Phantom" and his relation-
ship with Lady Audiart.

The first half of the poem considers a subject not un-
like those dealt with in a *tenso*: how does one reciprocate
to a lady who "would that ill come unto him"? This is
the question Bertran struggles with as he tries to compose
"Na Audiart." The poem begins with a translation of
the first line of that stanza, a line that is translated in five
different ways throughout the poem, culminating with
the repetition of the line in Provençal that closes the
poem. Thus, the line serves as a sort of ground bass
around which the poem is constructed. It is also the
epigraph to the poem, in a slightly altered form:

> N'Audiartz, si bem vol mal,
> vuolh quem don de sas faissos,
> quelh estai genliazos
> e car es entieira,
> c'anc nois frais
> s'amors nis vols en biais;[15]

> Of Audiart at Malemort,
> Though she with a full heart
> Wish me ill,
> I'd have her form that's laced
> So cunningly,
> Without blemish, for her love
> Breaks not nor turns aside.   (*P*, 106:1914)

[15] Text in Stimming, *Bertran de Born*, p. 149.

Again we see the addition of a place name ("at Male-
mort") for the sake of clarification and the sort of elabo-
ration ("with a full heart" and "that's laced / So cun-
ningly") witnessed in our discussion of this translation
in Chapter I.

Throughout the first half of "Na Audiart" there is a
constant movement between Bertran's recognition of Au-
diart's disdain for him ("Que be-m vols mal") and his
desire to praise her beauty, until finally a relationship be-
tween these two is suggested. Audiart is eulogized at
some length in terms suggested, not by Bertran's poem,
but by Pound's interpretation of it.[16] For example, we
have seen that the phrase "that's laced / So cunningly"
is an addition of Pound's. The Provençal simply states:
"I want her to give me her form / For it is a gracious out-
fit for her." Pound expands his translation, "that's laced /
So cunningly," to:

> Where thy bodice laces start
> As ivy fingers clutching through
> Its crevices,
> > Audiart, Audiart . . .   (P, 8)

He returns to this after a momentary pass to Miels-de-
Ben:

> Having praised thy girdle's scope
> How the stays ply back from it . . .

Then, as Witemeyer has pointed out, Bertran's "atten-
tion moves systematically downward from her bodice to
her girdle and finally to 'Where thy torse and limbs are
met.' Picking up the word 'entiera' from the Provençal
. . . De Born applies it genitally: ' 'Cause never a flaw

---

[16] See Chapter 1, pp. 33-39.

was there.' "[17] Bertran's interest in Audiart is obviously
not spiritual, and yet his viewpoint is that of a voyeur,
rather than a lusty participant in the pleasures she could
offer him. His response here is significant: instead of at-
tempting to establish a physical relationship with Audi-
art, he is content to chronicle her beauty in the "rose and
gold" of the manuscript, and to send her a "word kiss"!
Thus Pound's persona shies away from sexual contact
at the moment when it seems most natural, preferring in-
stead to seek refuge in his art.

The final line of this section, "Oh, till thou come
again," is a variation on a line from "Dompna Pois" ("tro
vos me siatz renduda"), which in the Provençal refers
to the poet's hope that Maent will be returned to him.
Pound takes this line, translates it, interprets it figura-
tively, and applies it to Audiart. For here, as Pound makes
clear in a footnote, he is not speaking of a return in a
physical sense, but rather of the lady's reincarnation at a
later date. Pound often interprets material in this way,
and the theme of metempsychosis is a common one in his
verse. In the section that follows we view Audiart in
another incarnation. Witemeyer has suggested that these
lines are governed "by the spirit of Ronsard's sonnet,
'Quand vous serez bien vieille,' "[18] but in fact they are
much closer to the poem that preceded it in *A Lume
Spento*, "In Epitathium Eius." Here we *are* near the
phantom of "Dompna puois" who represents a platonic
ideal of beauty, aspects of whom are embodied in a num-
ber of different women:

> Servant and Singer, Troubadour
> That for his loving, loved each fair face more

[17] Witemeyer, *The Poetry of Ezra Pound*, p. 77.
[18] *Ibid.*

54

Than craven sluggard can his life's one love,

Dowered with love, "whereby the sun doth move
And all the stars."
They called him fickle that the lambent flame
Caught "Bicé" dreaming in each new-blown name,

And loved all fairness though its hidden guise
Lurked various in half an hundred eyes;

That loved the essence though each casement bore
A different semblance than the one before.

(ALS, 20)

The concept of the artist presented here has an obvious applicability to the Bertran of both "Dompna Pois" and "Na Audiart." Here Pound speaks wryly of Audiart's reincarnation in a new and different "casement":

And being bent and wrinkled, in a form
That hath no perfect limning, when the warm
Youth dew is cold
Upon thy hands, and thy old soul
Scorning a new, wry'd casement,
Churlish at seemed misplacement,
Finds the earth as bitter
As now seems it sweet ...

(P, 9)

Notice too the play on "limning," which retains its etymological relationship to the illuminated manuscript Pound refers to above.

In the final lines Pound develops Audiart's reaction to her new situation, and the perspective in which it puts her current beauty. Bertran seems to take a bitter pride in the knowledge that it is only through his verse that her present beauty can be preserved. Her ultimate recognition of this will "soften" her, and make her realize that it is because of her beauty that he has forgiven her:

> Broken of ancient pride,
> Thou shalt then soften,
> Knowing, I know not how,
> Thou were once she
> > Audiart, Audiart
> For whose fairness one forgave
> > Audiart,
> Audiart,
> > Que be-m vols mal.   (P, 9)

"Na Audiart," then, presents the results of a meditation on the significance of one stanza of "Dompna Pois." Pound's development of the persona here is quite sophisticated: Speaking through Bertran, he creates a Provençal poem in English that is both a "criticism by translation" and a "criticism in a new composition" (LE, 74-75:1934).

A somewhat complementary use of Bertran as persona can be seen in "Sestina: Altaforte" (1909). Here Pound is drawing largely upon Dante's description of Bertran, and the image one gets from "Be·m platz lo gais temps de Pascor," where the troubadour praises at great length the excitement of combat. Bertran is not seen as a lover, but simply as a belligerent warrior, a "stirrer up of strife."

In "How I Began" (1913), Pound has given an account of his composition of this work: "I had had De Born on my mind. I had found him untranslatable. Then it occurred to me that I might present him in this manner. I wanted the curious involution and recurrence of the Sestina. I knew more or less of the arrangement. I wrote the first strophe and then went to the Museum to make sure of the right order of permutations. . . . I did the rest of the poem at a sitting. Technically it is one of my best,

56

though a poem on such a theme could never be very important."[19]

He employs the sestina developed by Arnaut Daniel, which he has called "a thin sheet of flame folding and infolding upon itself" (SR, 27). Thus, he is not only using Provençal subject matter here, but a Provençal form as well. With the exception of two lines (21-22, where the end words are reversed), and the envoi (where only four of the six end words are repeated), Pound follows Daniel's scheme exactly. It is clearly a very demanding pattern and Pound's poem is a tour de force.

The strident opening establishes a tone that never slackens, as the reader is confronted with a Bertran quite unlike the character presented in "Na Audiart." In the epigraph Pound facetiously asks us to consider whether Dante's judgment of Bertran was correct, and then proceeds to portray him unequivocally as a bloodthirsty warrior. As other commentators have pointed out, Pound creates an immediate audience for the dramatic monologue by addressing Papiols, Bertran's jongleur and the traditional subject of the envoy, at the outset.[20] Both stanzas I and VI invoke Papiols' music, and, by extension, praise the music and artistic beauty of armed conflict. Bertran also alludes in stanza VI to his war with Richard Coeur-de-Lion, and thus Pound reminds us of Dante's condemnation of Bertran for setting brother against brother (i.e., the "young King" and Richard). Stanzas II and IV introduce the natural strife of the elements. In

[19] Ezra Pound, "How I Began," T. P.'s Weekly (June 6, 1913), p. 707. Reprinted in Ezra Pound: Perspectives, Essays in honor of his eightieth birthday, ed. with an introduction by Noel Stock (Chicago, 1965), p. 1.

[20] De Nagy, The Poetry of Ezra Pound, pp. 125-126; Witemeyer, The Poetry of Ezra Pound, p. 75.

his monomania, Bertran sees war everywhere, in the normal life of the elements and in the passing of night and the coming of dawn. The implication, important in terms of Pound's characterization of Bertran, is that warfare is a natural condition. Thus those who prefer peace to war (stanzas III and V) are unnatural and should be condemned (here in the language of "Un sirventes on motz no falh"). The envoy unequivocally presents Bertran as a bloodthirsty warrior, and his two invocations to "hell" are an ironic reminder of Dante's later placement of him.

Pound uses the repetitions of the sestina very effectively in his characterization of Bertran. Unlike Daniel, who had chosen end words that change in meaning from verse to verse, Pound's end words are relatively inflexible, and simply produce a hollow echo with each repetition. Indeed, the limitations of Pound's end words tend to flatten this aspect of Bertran's character. Although the form is complicated, the poem is not: one might even say that the complexity of the form is used to underline the simplicity of the character being portrayed. Yet, although Bertran is not complex here, he is convincing, for Pound succeeds in getting inside the persona, and in speaking through him very effectively.

The two aspects of Bertran's character that Pound has developed separately in the two preceding poems are brought together in "Near Perigord" (1915). In this work Pound attempts to relate Bertran's interest in war to his interest in love, and tries to resolve issues not unlike those presented in "Marvoil" and "Piere Vidal Old." Pound proposes the "riddle": Was "Dompna Pois" simply a love poem, or was it a strategic maneuver? Was Bertran primarily a love poet, or a man of war? In order to answer these questions, Pound employs a meth-

od he had begun to develop in the earlier personae, and
that he later refined upon in *The Cantos*.

The first section of "Near Perigord" presents the "his-
torical facts," based partly on the *vida* ("Uc de St. Circ's
statement that Bertrans de Born was in love with the
Lady Maent, wife of Sir Tairiran of Montaignac and
that when she turned him out he wrote a canzon, *Domp-
na . . .*"),[21] partly on Dante's characterization of Bertran,
partly on "evidence" from Bertran's own poems, and
partly on historical and literary precedents. The problem
that this material presents is noted at the outset:

> You'd have men's hearts up from the dust
> And tell their secrets, Messire Cino,
> Right enough? Then read between the lines
>   of Uc St. Circ,
> Solve me the riddle, for you know the tale.   (P, 151)

Pound used the pseudonym "Cino" for several of his early
poems, and the opening lines could certainly refer to his
epigraph to "Sestina: Altaforte":

> Dante Alighieri put this man in hell for that
>   he was a stirrer up of strife.
> Eccovi!
> Judge ye!
> Have I dug him up again?   (P, 28)

Indeed, all of Pound's Provençal personae have been "dug
up again," as we have seen. Nowhere is his intention in
these poems more clearly stated than here. The "riddle"
he speaks of is, of course, his own invention, and already
suggests an interpretation of the material being presented.

[21] Ezra Pound, "On 'Near Perigord,'" *Poetry*, VII, 3 (Dec.
1915), p. 143.

The first piece of "evidence" is the *canso* by Bertran, which Pound summarizes in several lines: "Maent, I love you, you have turned me out. . . ." The phrase "I love you" appears nowhere in "Dompna Pois," and thus Pound's "evidence" is biased at the outset. But although this may be a love poem, the question of Bertran's duplicity remains. In a note published in *Poetry*, Pound explained: "As to the possibility of a political intrigue behind the apparent love poem we have no evidence save that offered by my own observation of the geography of Perigord and Limoges."[22] The word "apparent" gives Pound away, as does his identification in his translation of "Dompna Pois" of the ladies by castle, so that the reader will not miss the possibility that the poem sets one kingdom against another. Certainly the poem is permeated with a powerful feeling for the shape and contours of the physical environment; in this respect it resembles "Provincia Deserta" (1915), with which it shares many descriptive details. Pound noticed that Altafort was flanked by the castle belonging to Maent's husband, who with his brother,[23] controlled most of that area. Perhaps, then, there is a justification for the Bertran of "Sestina: Altaforte"? Being surrounded by more powerful lords, he simply had no choice but to provoke them to fight each other. Dante's punishment of De Born in the ninth ring of Hell would seem to be a literal equivalent of De Born's activity on earth:

> And our En Bertrans was in Altafort,
> Hub of the wheel, the stirrer-up of strife,

[22] *Ibid.*, pp. 145-146.

[23] Pound incorrectly refers to Maent's husband's brother-in-law. See K. K. Ruthven, *A Guide to Ezra Pound's "Personae" (1926)* (Berkeley and Los Angeles, 1969), p. 178.

As caught by Dante in the last wallow of hell—
The headless trunk "that made its head a lamp,"
For separation wrought out separation,
And he who set the strife between brother and brother
And had his way with the old English king,
Viced in such torture for the "counterpass."

(P, 151)

Pound quotes two lines from Bertran's "Be·m platz lo gais temps de Pascor"[24] to support this characterization: "Baron, metetz en gatge / Castels e vilas e ciutatz," which he translates as "Pawn your castles, lords! Let the Jews pay," a vivid but distorted rendering of the Provençal. The result of Bertran's stirring up of war was his defeat and the legendary conversation between him and the English King (recorded in Bertran's *razo*, or critical biography). But the authenticity of this "fact" eludes us, for "that, maybe, never happened!"[25]

The poem continues to interweave literary "evidence" with geographical "evidence":

Is it a love poem? Did he sing of war?
Is it an intrigue to run subtly out,
Born of a jongleur's tongue, freely to pass
Up and about and in and out the land,
Mark him a craftsman and a strategist?

[24] Text in Stimming, *Bertran de Born*, p. 228.

[25] In his explanatory note in *Poetry* ("On 'Near Perigord,'" p. 146), Pound stated: "The traditional scene of Bertrans before King Henry Plantagenet is well recounted in Smith's *Troubadours at Home*. It is vouched for by many old manuscripts and seems as well authenticated as most Provençal history, though naturally there are found the usual perpetrators of 'historic doubt.'" Pound seems here to be such a "perpetrator of 'historic doubt.'"

(St. Leider had done as much as Polhonaç
Singing a different stave, as closely hidden.)
Oh, there is a precedent, legal tradition,
To sing one thing when your song means another,
"*Et albirar ab lor bordon—*"
Foix' count knew that.   (*P*, 153)

Pound's intentions are clarified by a statement of his
in "Troubadours—Their Sorts and Conditions" (1913):
"No student of the period can doubt that the involved
forms, and the veiled meanings in the 'trobar clus,' grew
out of living conditions, and that these songs played a
very real part in love intrigue and in the intrigue preced-
ing warfare. The time had no press and no theatre. If
you wish to make love to women in public, and out loud,
you must resort to subterfuge; and Guillaume St. Leider
even went so far as to get the husband of his lady to do
the seductive singing" (*LE*, 94). This, of course, was im-
plicit in "Marvoil" and "Piere Vidal Old," and Pound
actually documents his contention that a poem may say
one thing and mean another. The line by the Count of
Foix, "et albirar ab lor bordon," is translated by Pound
in the article cited above as "and sing not all they have
in mind." Moreover, it is obvious that the jongleur, with
his easy access to the castles of the region, could be of
strategic importance to his master, both in questions of
war and love. In *Flamenca*, a work that Pound discusses
briefly in *The Spirit of Romance*, there is a reference to
the role of the jongleur as a secret messenger between the
two lovers. Just before their separation, Flamenca says
to Guillaume:

Et antretan mandares mi
Per alcun adreg pellegri

Per message o per juglar,
Tot vostr' esser e vostr' afar.[26]

[And meanwhile send me
By some distinguished pilgrim
By messenger or by jongleur,
News of your state and condition.]

There is thus ample historical precedent for this type of activity, although, as Pound knows, we can ultimately do no more than conjecture about it.

Pound continues to weigh these possibilities throughout this section:

He loved this lady in castle Montagnac?
....

And Maent failed him? Or saw through
the scheme?
....

And every one half jealous of Maent?
He wrote the catch to pit their jealousies
Against her; give her pride in them?
....

Is it a love poem? Did he sing of war?
....

Maent, Maent, and yet again Maent,
Or war and broken heaumes and politics?

(P, 152-154)

The question cannot be resolved by simply collating documents and examining sources. At the end of the section we are no closer to Bertran's intention than at the outset, although Pound has defined the nature of the riddle he is presenting more clearly.

The second section begins, "End fact. Try fiction." Here we find a fictional recreation of Bertran as he sits

[26] Text in *Le Roman de Flamenca*, ed., Paul Meyer (Paris, 1901), ll. 6,787-6,790.

in his castle composing his *canso*. He completes the poem and sends Papiols through the courts with it. Arrimon Luc D'Esparo, hearing it at Ventadour, "guesses beneath, sends word to Coeur-de-Lion," and so Bertran is attacked and defeated. Just as the reader begins to feel that this possibility may answer the riddle, Pound presents an alternative: "Or no one sees it, and En Bertrans prospered?" Again, we cannot even be sure of Bertran's defeat.

Next we have a sort of *tenso* between Arnaut Daniel and Richard Coeur-de-Lion, as they discuss the merits of Bertran's poetry and the "riddle" it presents:

> Plantagenet puts the riddle: "Did he love her?"
> And Arnaut parries: "Did he love your sister?
> True, he has praised her, but in some opinion
> He wrote that praise only to show he had
> The favour of your party; had been well received."
>
> "You knew the man."
>   "*You* knew the man."
> "I am an artist, you have tried both métiers."
> "You were born near him."
>   "Do we know our friends?"
> "Say that he saw the castles, say that he loved
>   Maent!"
> "Say that he loved her, does it solve the riddle?"
> End the discussion . . .   (P, 155-156)

His contemporaries, in this "fictional" re-creation, can do no more than assert that perhaps the two aspects of the "riddle" are not mutually exclusive. But if certainty eludes them, how can we decide, after "six hundred years?"[27]

[27] Pound had considered this point several years earlier in "Osiris, IV," *New Age*, X, 8 (Dec. 21, 1911), p. 179, where he

The section ends with another reference to Dante's judgment of De Born. In a lovely translation of a passage from Canto XXVIII of the *Inferno*, Pound presents Bertran among the "sowers of scandal and schism." Pound has condensed Dante's twenty-five lines into six, and his deletions and transformations are of considerable interest. A prose translation of the entire passage appears in *The Spirit of Romance*:

"Certainly I saw, and to this hour I seem to see, a trunk going headless, even as went the others of that dismal throng, and it held the severed head by the hair, swinging in his hand like a lantern, which looking upon us, said, 'Ah me!'

"Of itself it made itself a lamp, and they were two in one and one in two (He who governeth the universe knows how this can be).

"When he was just at the foot of the bridge, it raised its arm with the face full towards us, to bring near its words, which were; Behold the pain grievous, thou who, breathing goest looking upon the dead; see if there be pain great as this is, and that thou may'st bear tidings of me, know me, Bertrans de Born; who gave never comfort to the young king. I made the father and the son rebels between them; Achitophel made not more of Absalom and David by his ill-wandering goads. Because I have sundered persons so joined (in kinship), I bear my brain parted, *Lasso!* from its beginning, which is this

states: " 'Her love is as the laurel or the broom is.' The compliment is here given, presumably, to Mona Laura and the Lady Plantagenest [sic] . . . or it is, maybe, only in homage to the loyalty of Richard himself. After seven centuries one cannot be too explicit in the unravelling of personal allusion."

torse. Thus is the counterpass observed in me"[28] (*SR*, 45).

Compare this with Pound's version:

> Surely I saw, and still before my eyes
> Goes on that headless trunk that bears for light
> Its own head swinging, gripped by the dead hair,
> And like a swinging lamp that says, "Ah me!
> I severed men, my head and heart
> Ye see here severed, my life's 'counterpart.' "

> (*P*, 156)

The last two lines of Pound's translation are highly interpretative. Dante has Bertran's head separated from his body as an expression of "il contrapasso," or what Pound earlier in the poem calls the "counterpass" and elsewhere "the laws of external justice" (*SR*, 127). However, Pound's version emphasizes a separation of "head and heart"; and thus he is interpreting Dante to support his belief that Bertran was torn between his devious strategy (his "head") and his love for Maent (his "heart"). This division is underscored by Pound's translation of "il contrapasso" as "my life's counterpart."

In the third part we examine this "division" in another context. Among the lines that Pound dropped from his abbreviated translation of Dante is that which forms the epigraph to this section: "And they were two in one and one in two." This epigraph refers both to the separation of "head and heart" noted above and, as Thomas E. Connolly has observed, to Bertran's relationship with

[28] Translator unidentified. This is not "the Temple translation of Dante which I have in the main used where there is no indication to the contrary" (*SR*, 9).

Maent.[29] The two lines with which this section originally began clarify Pound's intentions:

> I loved a woman. The stars fell from heaven.
> And always our two natures were in strife.[30]

Even with the deletion of these two lines, the other references to Dante make the parallel quite clear. The results of Bertran's "strife" at the "hub of the wheel" in Altafort (Part I) and his "strife" with Maent, governed by "the great wheels in heaven" (Part III) are the same, "for separation wrought out separation":

> And the great wheels in heaven
> Bore us together . . . surging . . . and apart . . .
> Believing we should meet with lips and hands,
>
>> High, high and sure . . . and then the
>>   counterthrust:
> 'Why do you love me? Will you always love me?
> But I am like the grass, I can not love you.'
> Or, 'Love, and I love and love you,
> And hate your mind, not *you*, your soul, your hands.'
>
> (P, 157)

This too is Dante's justice, "the counterthrust": just as we can never understand Bertran's motives, he himself can never know if Maent loves him. All he can be sure of is that he has been repaid in kind for his divisiveness.

However, there is "still the knot, the first knot, of Maent" which Pound unties in the final lines of the poem:

[29] Thomas E. Connolly, "Ezra Pound's 'Near Perigord': The Background of a Poem," p. 116.

[30] Ezra Pound, "Two Poems," *Poetry*, VII, 3 (Dec. 1915), p. 118. Reprinted in Ruthven, *A Guide to Ezra Pound's "Personae" (1926)*, p. 183.

> There shut up in his castle, Tairiran's
> She who had nor ears nor tongue save in her hands,
> Gone—ah, gone—untouched, unreachable!
> She who could never live save through one person,
> She who could never speak save to one person,
> And all the rest of her a shifting change,
> A broken bundle of mirrors . . . !

Here Maent is a being whose existence is defined solely through the person and art of Bertran de Born. If, of course, the "real" Maent can be interpreted and preserved only through the achievement of a poet like Bertran, then the "real" Bertran (or Peire Vidal, or Arnaut de Mareuil) can exist only through the art of a poet like Dante or Pound. What was implicit in "Marvoil" and "Piere Vidal Old"—that only an artist like Pound is capable of recreating the real personality of the poet, which usually remains hidden from the public by the facade of his poems—is strongly affirmed here.

In a very important sense, Pound's poem is a "Descant on a theme by Dante," to paraphrase the title of one of his other acts of homage. Throughout the poem Pound shows that Dante's interpretation of Bertran's character was correct. Pound gives further support for Dante's judgment of Bertran, and shows that Dante's punishment was in fact effective even before Bertran's death. Bertran separated brothers, and in so doing was separated from Maent. The reason for this, Pound suggests (and this is as close as we can get to answering the "riddle"), was that Bertran himself was the victim of internal strife. Pound develops this theme through repetition—a technique that becomes very important in *The Cantos*. As we have seen, he had experimented with this technique as early as 1908 in "Na Audiart," where the Provençal line "que be-m vols mal" recurs in a number of translations and becomes the organizing principle of the poem. In "Near Perigord" Pound considers the meaning of "il contrapasso," and explores the nature of this "justice" in all possible contexts. The reader discovers that Dante's justice, like one of Pound's definitions of poetry, is a "sort of inspired mathematics" (*SR*, 14), where the punishment = the crime. Bertran, torn in life between his head and his heart, finds this to be his ultimate fate.

Taken as a group, these poems reveal the qualities in Provence that attracted Pound, qualities that became a permanent part of his world view. Moreover, his methods of using historical materials here prefigure his use of similar material in *The Cantos*. Pound resuscitates the past so that historical figures become his contemporaries: as Eliot has written, Pound "has grasped certain things in Provence . . . which are permanent in human nature. . . . When he deals with antiquities, he extracts the essentially living. . . . But this does not mean that he is antiquarian or parasitical on literature. Any scholar can see Arnaut Daniel or Guido Cavalcanti as literary figures; only Pound can see them as living beings."[31]

[31] Introduction to *Ezra Pound: Selected Poems*, pp. 11-12.

Chapter III

TOWARDS AN EMPYREAN OF PURE LIGHT:
The Radiant Medieval World

The light became her grace and dwelt among
Blind eyes and shadows that are formed as men;
Lo, how the light doth melt us into song . . .
                    "Ballatetta"

A little light, like a rushlight
                    to lead back to splendour.
            "Canto cxvi"

IN the period from 1910 to 1912, the medieval world
became firmly established as the upper pole of Pound's
cosmos. In *Provença* (1910) and *Canzoni* (1911), Pound
defined the contours of this world and developed the ten-
sion noted in "Piere Vidal Old" between the vibrant
unity of the medieval world and the sterility of the pres-
ent "age gone lax." We have already considered the ideals
Pound attributed to the troubadour poets in his early per-
sonae and translations: what distinguishes his work in
these two volumes is his conscious adaptation of a con-
cept of love that had its origins in Provence and was fully
developed by the Italian poets of the *dolce stil nuovo*.

70

Thomas G. Bergin has noted that "Dante's Beatrice is clearly outlined in the lady of the troubadours,"[1] and he substantiates this by quoting a poem by Guilhem de Peitieus, the first troubadour. As we noticed in Chapters I and II, the Provençal conception of love appealed greatly to Pound. During the two centuries that separated Guilhem de Peitieus from Dante, Provençal poetry showed, in H. J. Chaytor's words, "an increasing refinement and delicacy of sentiment . . . the later troubadours gradually dissociated their love from the object which had aroused it: among them, love is no longer sexual passion; it is rather the motive to great works, to self-surrender, to the winning an honourable name as courtier and poet."[2] For Chaytor (whose works were well known by Pound),[3] Sordello was an important poet largely because he represented a transitional stage between the Provençal and Tuscan views of love. In his poetry love has become "rather a mystical idea than a direct affection for a particular lady: the lover is swayed by a spiritual and intellectual ideal, and the motive of physical attraction recedes to the background. The cause of love, however, remains unchanged: love enters through the eyes; sight is delight."[4]

Although Pound's early work bore evidence of his tacit acceptance of this notion of love, it did not become the cornerstone of his love ethic until he had immersed himself in the poetry of Guido Guinizelli, Guido Caval-

[1] Thomas G. Bergin, *An Approach to Dante* (London, 1965), p. 46.

[2] Chaytor, *The Troubadours of Dante*, pp. xxi-xxii.

[3] Pound studied this book under William P. Shepherd at Hamilton College.

[4] Chaytor, *The Troubadours*, p. 105.

canti, Dante, and the medieval philosophers who influenced them (in Pound's view, Richard of St. Victor and Robert Grosseteste). Following his overt discovery of this concept of *Amor* in the Tuscan poets, Pound traced it to its beginnings in Provence: "In the Trecento the Tuscans are busy with their *phantastikon*," he wrote. "In Provence we may find preparation for this" (*SR*, 93). This love, exemplified by Dante's deification of Beatrice, is Neo-Platonic in nature, and becomes realized through the worship of an ideal, embodied in a lady of great beauty. She is almost always an ethereal being surrounded by a brilliant light symbolizing her *virtù*. Early Tuscan poetry is characterized by this spiritualization of the lady, and by a philosophical consideration of the nature of love. As Pound stated in *The Spirit of Romance*: "The art of the troubadours meets with philosophy at Bologna and a new era of lyric poetry is begun" (*SR*, 101).

Pound's initial interest in early Tuscan poetry was precisely in those poems which developed the qualities of the lady mentioned above. At this point (c. 1910), he was scarcely concerned with the conceptualizing that distinguishes "Donna mi prega," a work that he classified as late as 1913 as belonging to "the dullest of the schools, set to explaining the nature of love and its effects" (*LE*, 103). His 1910 version of "Chi è questa," published in *Provença*, poses a question similar to that asked of Guido Cavalcanti by Guido Orlandi: Cavalcanti's answer was the elaborately conceived intellectual argumentation of "Donna mi prega"; Pound's answer is simply "O mind give place! / What holy mystery e'er was noosed in thought?" It is interesting to note that Pound did not immediately assimilate this tradition in its entirety, but first selected from among the early poems, where he

72

found a concept of the lady implicit in the Provençal poetry he had been studying so closely.

The earliest of these poets to interest Pound was Guinizelli, to whom J. E. Shaw has attributed the "motive of dazzling light surrounding the figure of the lady, preceding her, illuminating all about her, [and] shining from her face and eyes."[5] Pound translated two of Guinizelli's poems completely in *The Spirit of Romance*, and they are important both for their own merits and for their influence on Cavalcanti. The first of these is "Vedut' ho la lucente stella diana":

> I have seen the shining star of the dawn
> Appearing ere the day yieldeth its whiteness.
> It has taken upon itself the form of a human face,
> Above all else meseems it gives splendor.
> A face of snow, color of the ivy-berry,
> The eyes are brilliant, gay, and full of love,
> And I do not believe that there is a Christian
>   maid in the world
> So full of fairness or so valorous.
> Yea, I am so assailed of her worth,
> With such cruel battling of sighs,
> That I am not hardy to return before her;
> Thus may she have cognizance of my desires:
> That without speaking, I would be her servitor
> For naught save the pity that she might have of
>   my anguish.   (SR, 105)

The opening lines develop the dawn light of the Provençal *alba* in a way that Pound would have found very attractive. It is as though this radiant virtue were seeking

5 J. E. Shaw, *Guido Cavalcanti's Theory of Love: The Canzone d'Amore and Other Related Problems* (Toronto, 1949), p. 117.

embodiment, and indeed the poem does fulfill this function. Notice that the source of love is in the eyes, as Cavalcanti later emphasized in "Donna mi prega." The qualities Pound has praised in this poem are the "preciseness of the description" and the "clarity of imaginative vision" (*SR*, 105). "The Tuscan poetry," he has stated, "is ... of a time when the seeing of visions was considered respectable, and the poet takes delight in definite portrayal of his vision" (*SR*, 105). Thus Pound is impressed with both the content of the vision, and with Guinizelli's search for *le mot juste* to describe it. This visionary quality can be applied equally well to an actual lady, as Pound's translation of the next poem demonstrates:[6]

> I wish with truth to speak my Lady's praise,
> And liken her to rose and gilly flower,
> More than the dawn star's grace her splendor is.
> The green stream's marge is like her, and the air,
> And all her colors are yellow flowers and red.
> Gold and silver and rich joys become more rarified, [sic],
> Yea, Love himself meseems refined through her.
>
> She goes her way adorned so graciously
> That pride forsakes whom she graces with greeting.
> Yea, he betrays our faith who creeds her not.
> No man impure may venture near to her.
> Yet would I tell you of a greater worth:
> There is no man whose evil thoughts do not
>   cease a little while before she appears.
>
> (*SR*, 106)

Here too the "dawn star" is seen as the epitome of great splendor and beauty; by exceeding this, the lady becomes

[6] A line is missing from the octave in all printed editions of this text.

TOWARDS AN EMPYREAN OF PURE LIGHT

an almost divine figure. So perfect is she that "love . . .
[is] . . . refined through her." Moreover, as Guinizelli
states in the sestet, one is made a better person merely by
coming into her presence.

The influence of this concept of the beloved on Caval-
canti can readily be seen by turning to "Chi è questa,"
a poem of such importance for Pound that he has trans-
lated it in four very different versions. Shaw cites this po-
em and three others by Cavalcanti ("Avete 'n voi," "Pos-
so de gli occhi," and "Veggio ne gli occhi") as showing
Guinizelli's influence, and he suggests that this way of
presenting the lady "is perhaps a poetical reflection of
the doctrine of metaphysical light familiar to both po-
ets."[7] This was a doctrine advanced by Robert Grosse-
teste, who held that "just as physical light is the basis of
all material forms, so the light of divine illumination is
the foundation of our knowledge of intelligible things."[8]
Pound's discussion of the final line of Cavalcanti's "Bal-
late" is important in this context. He translates it as "Then
shalt thou see her virtue risen in heaven," and states:

"Thus 'her' presence, his Lady's, corresponds with the
ascendancy of the star of that heaven which corresponds
to her particular emanation or potency. Likewise,
       Vedrai la sua virtù nel ciel salita.'
"Thou shalt see the rays of this emanation going up
to heaven as a slender pillar of light, or, more strictly in
accordance with the stanza preceding: thou shalt see
depart from her lips her subtler body, and from that a
still subtler form ascends and from that a star, the body
of pure flame surrounding the source of the *virtù*, which
will declare its nature" (*T*, 19:1912).

[7] Shaw, *Guido Cavalcanti*, p. 117.
[8] Julius R. Weinberg, *A Short History of Medieval Philosophy*
(Princeton, 1964), p. 160.

75

Thus the light that emanates from the lady defines her whole being, and serves as a source of illumination (both literally and figuratively) for those who come into her presence:

Who is she coming, drawing all men's gaze,
Who makes the air one trembling clarity
Till none can speak but each sighs piteously
Where she leads Love adown her trodden ways?

Ah God! The thing she's like when her glance strays,
Let Amor tell. 'Tis no fit speech for me.
Mistress she seems of such great modesty
That every other woman were called "Wrath."

No one could ever tell the charm she hath
For toward her all the noble Powers incline,
She being beauty's godhead manifest.

Our daring ne'er before held such high quest;
But ye! There is not in you so much grace
That we can understand her rightfully.[9]

The lady is a semi-divine figure ("beauty's godhead manifest") moving with precision and brilliance. Love emanates from her glance (as in the Guinizelli poem cited above), and all men become powerless in her presence. She is the apotheosis of a type of beauty that for Pound characterizes the medieval world—that "radiant world

[9] This version was first published in "Osiris, III," *New Age*, x, 7 (Dec. 14, 1911), p. 155, and reprinted in *The Sonnets and Ballate of Guido Cavalcanti* (p. 15), with an alternative translation of the last five lines. See also *The Spirit of Romance* (p. 111) for a translation of the first four lines strongly influenced by Rossetti's version and *The Translations of Ezra Pound* (p. 39) for Pound's final version (1934) of this poem.

where one thought cuts through another with clean edge, a world of moving energies . . . magnetisms that take form, that are seen, or that border the visible, the matter of Dante's *paradiso*" (*LE*, 154). It is this world with its clarity and brilliant luminosity that becomes the basis of Pound's paradise as well.

In the above paragraphs we have attempted to elaborate upon the "phantastikon" of the Tuscans, and to account for its great appeal to Pound. As he became increasingly involved with early Italian poetry, through his work on *The Spirit of Romance*, *The Sonnets and Ballate of Guido Cavalcanti*, and the poems in *Provença* and *Canzoni*, he began seeking antecedents for this spirit in Provençal poetry. Provençal poetry had, as we noted at the outset, been gradually changing in its presentation of love, although, of course, there was never a monolithic treatment of this subject. There did, however, seem to be a greater spiritualization of love among the later poets, although this was in part due to exterior forces, such as the Albigensian Crusade. Pound was well aware of this, but he took a much more mystical view of this transformation. "The cult of Provence," he wrote, "had been a cult of the emotions; and with it there had been some, hardly conscious, study of emotional psychology" (*SR*, 116). Pound's most exhaustive attempt to explain this "cult of the emotions" and to relate the highly developed "emotional psychology" that he so admired in Guinizelli, Cavalcanti, and Dante to its origins in Provence can be found in "Psychology and Troubadours," an article originally published in G.R.S. Mead's journal *The Quest* in 1912, and republished as Chapter v of *The Spirit of Romance*.

Pound's method in this article is to work backwards from his *donnée*—the development of *Amor* in Tuscany

77

—to the treatment of this subject in Provence, seeking whatever clues may support this theory:

"We must, however, take into our account a number of related things; consider, in following the clue of a visionary interpretation, whether it will throw light upon events and problems other than our own, and weigh the chances in favor of, or against, this interpretation. Allow for climate, consider the restless sensitive temper of our jongleur, and the quality of the minds which appreciated him. Consider what poetry was to become, within less than a century, at the hands of Guinicelli [sic], or of 'il nostro Guido' in such a poem as the *ballata*, ending: 'Vedrai la sua virtù nel ciel salita,' and consider the whole temper of Dante's verse. In none of these things singly is there any specific *proof*. Consider the history of the time, the Albigensian Crusade, nominally against a sect tinged with Manichean heresy, and remember how Provençal song is never wholly disjunct from pagan rites of May Day. [e.g., frequent Spring openings]. Provence was less disturbed than the rest of Europe by invasion from the North in the darker ages; if paganism survived anywhere it would have been, unofficially, in the Langue d'Oc. That the spirit was, in Provence, Hellenic is seen readily enough by anyone who will compare *The Greek Anthology* with the work of the troubadours. They have, in some way, lost the names of the gods and remembered the names of lovers" (*SR*, 90).

Pound proceeds from this series of hypotheses to postulate the existence of a mystic cult in which "a sheer love of beauty and a delight in the perception of it have . . . replaced all heavier emotion, [where] the thing has . . . become a function of the intellect" (*SR*, 90-91). The whole tradition of the *trobar clus*, in which the poets "sing not all they have in mind," is taken as evidence that the *canso* was "a ritual," making its "revelations to those who are already expert" (SR, 89). But Pound is not only concerned with the mystical content of these poems, he is also interested in their use of language. In defining "ecstasy" as "a glow arising from the exact nature of the perception" (SR, 91), Pound gives us a clue to the great emphasis he places on exact description. We have seen this in his discussion of Guinizelli and Cavalcanti, and later he says the same of Dante: "Dante's precision . . . comes from the attempt to reproduce exactly the thing which has been clearly seen" (SR, 126). Thus Pound finds antecedents in Provence for both the love visions of the Tuscans and the precision with which they describe them.

"Psychology and Troubadours" is one of Pound's more recondite essays; it would be of minor interest to us today if he had not put these theories into practice. But this visionary mysticism so prominent in Tuscan poetry confronts the Provençal tradition head on in a series of poems first published in Provença under the title of "Canzoniere" (Italian for "songbook"). Here, using Provençal verse forms that he identifies by poet and composition, as well as some Italian forms, Pound presents a series of poems that are clearly derived in content from early Italian poetry. These poems fall into two categories of criticism identified by Pound in "Date Line" (1934): they are both "criticism by exercise in the style of a given period" and "criticism in a new composition" (LE, 74-75). Thus they are stylistic exercises that frequently interpret themes found in the poems whose forms they employ.

"Canzon: The Yearly Slain,"[10] uses the form of Daniel's poem, "Sols sui qui sai lo sobrafan quem sortz."

[10] Pound consistently employs the Italian forms canzon, canzoni, rather than the Provençal canso.

As the epigraph indicates, Pound is following the example of Dante, who had also reflected upon and then imitated the Provençal forms. Pound quotes from *De Vulgari Eloquentia*, a work that he had studied thoroughly: "Et huiusmodi stantiae usus est fere in omnibus cantionibus suis Arnaldus Danielis et nos eum secut, sumus." ("This kind of stanza was used by Arnaut Daniel, in almost all of his Canzoni, and we have followed him in ours, beginning—"). Moreover, "The Yearly Slain" is "written in reply to [Frederic] Manning's 'Korè,'" and thus Pound is following a very popular medieval tradition: writing a poem that answers or amplifies the work of another poet. He is also uniting "Provençal song" and "pagan rites." However, the spirit of Pound's poem is very different from that of Manning's. For Manning, Persephone is an aged woman, slowly ushering in winter as she moves among the shadows:

> With slow reluctant feet and weary eyes
> And eyelids heavy with the coming sleep
> With small breasts lifted up in stress of sighs,
> She passed as shadows pass amid the sheep
> While the earth dreamed and only I was ware
> Of that faint fragrance blown from her soft hair.
>
> (*Pr*, 67)

Pound's Persephone is a young woman filled with vigor, whose departure, although devastating, is none the less beautiful:

> Ah! red-leafed time hath driven out the rose
> And crimson dew is fallen on the leaf
> Ere ever yet the cold white wheat be sown
> That hideth all earth's green and sere and red;
> The Moon-flower's fallen and the branch is bare,

80

Holding no honey for the starry bees;
The Maiden turns to her dark lord's demesne.

Fairer than Enna's field when Ceres sows
The stars of hyacinth and puts off grief,
Fairer than petals on May morning blown
Through apple-orchards where the sun hath shed
His brighter petals down to make them fair;
Fairer than these the Poppy-crowned One flees,
And Joy goes weeping in her scarlet train.

(Pr, 64-65)

Pound continues to describe the passing of Korè in the third stanza; it becomes evident that this evocation of nature is not of primary importance in itself, as in Manning's poem, but functions rather as a "background." Pound is closely following a precedent he had noticed earlier in Provençal poetry: ". . . in most Provençal poetry one finds nature in its proper place, i.e. as a background to the action, an interpretation of the mood; an equation, in other terms, or a 'metaphor by sympathy' for the mood of the poem" (SR, 31). The speaker in Manning's poem bemoans the passing of Korè, and "weep[s] until she come[s] again," but Pound goes much further, and sees this cycle of nature as a reflection of the temporal nature of man's love for woman:

Love that is born of Time and comes and goes!
Love that doth hold all noble hearts in fief!
As red leaves follow where the wind hath flown,
So all men follow Love when Love is dead . . .

(Pr, 65)

Pound then develops one of his most pessimistic statements on the nature of love:

81

Korè my heart is, let it stand sans gloze!
Love's pain is long, and lo, love's joy is brief!
My heart erst alway sweet is bitter grown;
As crimson ruleth in the good green's stead,
So grief hath taken all mine old joy's share
And driven forth my solace and all ease
Where pleasure bows to all-usurping pain.

Crimson the hearth where one last ember glows!
My heart's new winter hath no such relief,
Nor thought of Spring whose blossom he hath known
Hath turned him back where Spring is banished.
Barren the heart and dead the fires there,
Blow! O ye ashes, where the winds shall please,
But cry, "Love also is the Yearly Slain."

Be sped, my Canzon, through the bitter air!
To him who speaketh words as fair as these,
Say that I also know the "Yearly Slain."

(*Pr*, 66)

Obviously, the love being considered here is quite different from the force that permeates the other poems in this series. Here Pound is presenting a temporal love, not unlike the *fals' amors* of the troubadour poets. It is based on a sexuality unredeemed by any nobler vision. The memory of this experience is a source of bitterness, rather than nourishment, for the speaker. Important too is the fact that this love is associated not with a figure of radiance, but rather with Persephone, the queen of Hades. The significance of the season, mentioned earlier, can now be seen: unlike many Provençal lyrics, which begin with the promise of spring, this poem opens with the death of everything spring represents. Pound begins his sequence on a negative note, with an exposition of the dangers of *fals' amors*.

Two other poems in this sequence also employ verse forms of Daniel's: "Canzon: The Vision," like "Canzon: The Yearly Slain," uses the form of "Sols sui qui sai lo sobrafan quem sortz," and "Canzon: Of Incense" uses the form of "Doutz brais e critz." These two poems are presentations of *fin' amors*, and develop what Pound considers to be the implicit mystical content of the poems on which they are based. Both are examples of the "servants of Amor [seeing] visions" (*SR*, 91). Each poem chronicles a love perceived at a distance in time and space (an *amor de lonh*), and in each poem the lady is described in terms of the Tuscan poets. The atmosphere is more expressly medieval than in the other poems in the series, with metaphoric detail being chosen to create this mood. This is evident at once in "Canzon: Of Incense":

> Thy gracious ways,
> O Lady of my heart, have
> O'er all my thought their golden glamour cast;
> As amber torch-flames, where strange men-at-arms
> Tread softly 'neath the damask shield of night,
> Rise from the flowing steel in part reflected,
> So on my mailed thought that with thee goeth,
> Though dark the way, a golden glamour falleth.
>
> (*Pr*, 71)

Pound juxtaposes the type of medievalism he perceives in the *dolce stil nuovo* (the "golden glamour") with the Pre-Raphaelite medievalism of lines 3-6. Here too he has a problem with diction. Since the content (i.e., a mystical doctrine of love) is removed from the sphere of mundane everyday activities, Pound realizes that he must create a language to indicate this. At this point, however, he is still unable to do so; he falls back on the language of the

83

Victorian translators who had introduced him to these poets.

This same diction permeates "The Vision," giving a quaint quality to the mysticism and thereby making it very much a thing of the past:

> When new love plucks the falcon from his wrist,
> And cuts the gyve and casts the scarlet hood,
> Where is the heron heart whom flight avails?
> O quick to prize me Love, how suddenly
> From out the tumult truth hath ta'en his own,
> And in this vision is our past unrolled.
> Lo! With a hawk of light thy love hath caught me.
>
> (Pr, 77)

The sixth line of this stanza articulates an important aspect of much of Pound's love poetry: "And in this vision is our *past* unrolled." It is a poetry that continually looks backward and relives the moment of ecstasy. The mere recollection of a previous love sustains the poet in the present, and more than substitutes for an active participation in a living relationship. The same is true of "Canzon: Of Incense," as well as of some of the early personae, notably "Piere Vidal Old" and "Marvoil." Yet there is a difference here, for the mystical experience in "Canzon: Of Incense" and "Canzon: The Vision" is caused as much by the contemplation of an ideal beauty as by a sexual encounter. Having experienced such a moment, the poet finds everything that follows of lesser importance, as stanza IV of "The Vision" makes clear:

> And I shall get no peace from eucharist,
> Nor doling out strange prayers before the rood,

To match the peace that thine hands' touch entails;
Nor doth God's light match light shed over me
When they caught sunlight is about me thrown,
Oh, for the very ruth thine eyes have told,
Answer the rune this love of thee hath taught me.

(Pr, 77-78)

Nothing can replace this moment of past ecstasy, nor can it be experienced any way but directly:

After an age of longing had we missed
Our meeting and the dream, what were the good
Of weaving cloth of words? Were jeweled tales
An opiate meet to quell the malady
Of life unlived? In untried monotone
Were not the earth as vain, and dry, and old,
For thee, O Perfect Light, had I not sought thee?

(Pr, 78)

In speaking of the development of love through Provençal and Tuscan poetry, Pound states that "There is the final evolution of Amor by Guido and Dante, a new and paganish god, neither Erôs nor an angel of the Talmud" (SR, 92), and he seems to have reached a similar stage here.

The other two *cansos* that use Provençal forms have closer relationships to the poems upon which they are based. "Canzon: The Spear" employs the form of stanza used by Jaufre Rudel in "D'un amor de lonh." Like the poem by Rudel, as well as the two poems considered directly above, Pound's *canso* deals with someone who is separated from the object of his love. The "spear," a light symbolizing the lady's *virtù*, is so great that it not only

85

consoles the speaker for her absence but also leads his thoughts to where she is:

> 'Tis the clear light of love I praise
> That steadfast gloweth o'er deep waters,
> A clarity that gleams always.
> Though man's soul pass through troubled waters,
> Strange ways to him are opened.
> To shore the beaten ship is sped.
> If only love of light give aid.　　　　　　(*Pr*, 67)

Pound proceeds to develop the relationship between the speaker and the lady in an interesting manner. Unlike Rudel's poem, where a strong physical attraction exists, there is a complete absence of sexual contact. Not only are the two separated, but the speaker shows no longing for the physical presence of his beloved. What attracts him is the ideal she represents. Indeed, there is not even any indication that she is aware of his existence. The speaker realizes that he can never be physically reunited with his lady, and yet, like the speaker of "Marvoil," he pledges utter devotion to her and praises her in lofty terms. The penultimate stanza develops the Guinizellian light motif most beautifully:

> The light within her eyes, which slays
> Base thoughts and stilleth troubled waters,
> Is like the gold where sunlight plays
> Upon the still o'ershadowed waters.
> When anger is there minglèd
> There comes a keener gleam instead,
> Like flame that burns beneath thin jade.　　(*Pr*, 69)

Thus, although it deals with the same basic situation as

86

Rudel's poem, Pound's treatment of the subject is very different.

The "Canzon: To be Sung Beneath a Window" is also related to its source, Vidal's "Ab l'alen tir vas me l'aire." In Chapter II we examined Pound's translation of the first two stanzas of this poem, and one sees at a glance how Pound has adapted the principal image of Vidal's first stanza:

> [Vidal: Breathing I draw the air to me
> Which I feel coming from Provença . . .]

> Heart mine, art mine, whose embraces
> Clasp but wind that past thee bloweth?
> E'en this air so subtly gloweth,
> Guerdoned by thy sun-gold traces
> That my heart is half afraid
> For the fragrance on him laid;
> Even so love's might amazes!   (Pr, 69-70)

This is not an uncommon image in Provençal poetry. We have also noticed it in Pound's translation of the "Alba Innominata":

> Of that sweet wind that comes from Far-Away
> Have I drunk deep of my Beloved's breath . . .

However, the air that "so subtly gloweth" and the "sun-gold traces" define the nature of his beloved in a very special way. The second and third stanzas introduce another element not present in the Provençal, and that is the utter devotion of the poet to his mistress, which Pound contrasts with the *fals' amors* of the multitudes:

> Man's love follows many faces,
> My love only one face knoweth;

87

> Towards thee only my love floweth,
> And outstrips the swift stream's paces.   (*Pr*, 70)

This is a persistent theme in Pound's verse, one that has
no basis in Provençal or Tuscan poetry. In another poem,
"Guido Invites You Thus," Pound reveals his inability
to accept the possibility that Guido had ceased to love his
wife. Pound's love ethic requires complete fidelity and
devotion; inconstancy has no place there.

The final stanza develops another theme from Vidal,
the difficulty of properly praising the loved one:

> If my praise her grace effaces,
> Then 't is not my heart that showeth,
> But the skillness tongue that soweth
> Words unworthy of her graces.
> Tongue, that hath me so betrayed,
> Were my heart but here displayed,
> Then were sung her fitting praises.   (*Pr*, 70)

Thus Pound returns to the heart image with which he
began the poem, affirming that this alone is the source of
truthful perception. The only problem for the poet is to
free the heart so that it can properly articulate its emo-
tive content.

In these *cansos*, then, Pound develops his love ethic in
some interesting ways. The woman becomes increasingly
idealized; indeed, she becomes an ideal towards which
one strives, the object of one's quest. The lady is de-
scribed in terms of radiant light that not only symbolizes
her *virtù*, but that characterizes the essentials of this
medieval world. There is a noticeable lack of sexuality
in these poems. In the early poems, sexual consummation
became a moment of mystical ecstasy of such magnitude
that the remembrance of it was sufficient to sustain and

even nourish one for a lifetime. Now, however, ecstasy is "a glow arising from the exact nature of the perception" (*SR*, 91); this is a very different thing. As sexuality diminishes in importance, the relationship between the speaker and his lady begins to change. The *amor de lonh* theme becomes a persistent one, and yet, in spite of the separation, constancy and devotion are expected on the part of the speaker. The near deification of the woman indicates that Pound is well on his way to establishing his own "aristocracy of emotion . . . [or] . . . cult for the purgation of the soul by a refinement of, and lordship over, the senses" (*SR*, 90).

Taken together, these poems present a view of love that, as we have seen, is greatly influenced by the Provençal and Tuscan poets. Although Pound has not yet solved the problem of finding a suitable English for the Provençal, these poems represent a considerable stylistic achievement, for here he has succeeded in utilizing four different Provençal forms of the *canso*, in addition to the Italian forms of the sonnet, *canzon* and *ballata*. The poems unquestionably provided him with a discipline that helped strengthen his control of his craft, and they are quite a display of stylistic virtuosity. Although Pound dropped these poems from *Personae* (1926), T. S. Eliot included "Canzon: The Yearly Slain" and "Canzon: Of Incense" in his edition of Pound's *Selected Poems* (1928); they are among Pound's finest poems in a fixed form.

Apart from reprinting the "Canzoniere" series from *Provença*, *Canzoni* includes a number of original poems, among them the "Und Drang" sequence, which further develops the contrast between the barren present and the radiant medieval world. The sequence consists of twelve poems, the first six of which were dropped after republication in the American edition of *Lustra* (1917). These six depict the moral confusion of the pre-war world in an archaic, stilted language. Pound is not successful here; because of their banality of expression, these poems deserve to be deleted from the series. The second half of the sequence stresses the applicability of medieval values to the contemporary world, as an antidote to the conditions chronicled in the first six poems. Therefore, unless the reader is aware of the contrast Pound is attempting in the total sequence, he cannot fully understand the importance of the final poems.

The first of these poems is "The House of Splendour," a vision of the beloved described in the terms of Guinizelli and Cavalcanti, and an exposition of the power of her love. Most critics have assumed that II Corinthians is the source for this poem ("For we know that if our earthly house of this tabernacle were dissolved, we have a building of God, an house not made with hands, eternal in the heavens"),[11] but actually Pound seems to have been inspired by Pater's retelling of the "Cupid and Psyche" story in *Marius the Epicurean*.[12] Pound refers to this story in his discussion of myth in the first chapter of *The Spirit of Romance*, where he quotes the relevant paragraph from Pater. It is the vision first seen by Psyche, after having been carried away by Zephyrus to the place where she is to meet Cupid:

"And lo! a grove of mighty trees, with a fount of water, clear as glass, in the midst; and hard by the water, a dwelling-place, built not by human hands but

[11] See, for example, Witemeyer, *The Poetry of Ezra Pound*, p. 97, and Ruthven, *A Guide to Ezra Pound's "Personae"* (*1926*), p. 125.

[12] *Canzoni* also includes "Speech for Psyche in the Golden Book of Apuleius," similarly inspired by Pater.

by some divine cunning. One recognized, even at the entering, the delightful hostelry of a god. Golden pillars sustained the roof, arched most curiously in cedar-wood and ivory. The walls were hidden under wrought silver: —all tame and woodland creatures leaping forward to the visitor's gaze. Wonderful indeed was the craftsman, divine or half-divine, who by the subtlety of his art had breathed so wild a soul into the silver! The very pavement was distinct with pictures in goodly stones. In the glow of its precious metal the house is its own daylight, having no need of the sun. Well might it seem a place fashioned for the conversation of gods with men!"[13]

In *Marius the Epicurean*, Pater explains the attraction of this tale to Marius in terms which could apply equally well to Pound: ". . . this episode of Cupid and Psyche served to combine many lines of meditation, already familiar to Marius, into the ideal of a perfect imaginative love, centered upon a type of beauty entirely flawless and clean . . . The human body in its beauty, as the highest potency of all the beauty of material objects, seemed to him just then to be matter no longer, but, having taken celestial fire, to assert itself as indeed the true, though visible, soul or spirit in things."[14]

Pound would also like Pater's description of the creator of the house as a *"craftsman . . . who by the subtlety of his art had breathed so wild a soul into silver."* Indeed, both in language and mood, Pound's "House of Splendour" resembles Pater's version of Psyche's first view of her abode:

[13] Pound, *Spirit of Romance*, p. 17, Walter Pater, *Marius the Epicurean: His Sensations and Ideas*, Vol. I (London, 1907), p. 66.

[14] Pater, *Marius*, Vol. I, pp. 92-93.

'Tis Evanoe's,
A house not made with hands,
But out somewhere beyond the worldly ways
Her gold is spread, above, around, inwoven;
Strange ways and walls are fashioned out of it.

(P, 49)

Pound has made several significant alterations here: although Pater's palace has "golden pillars," it is chiefly made of ivory and wrought silver, cold elements that produce a self-sustaining glow, "having no need of the sun." Pound's palace is entirely of gold, but this metal is only a medium that catches the warm rays of the sun and is defined by them. Pound's concern with objects as mere media receiving their definition from the light passing through them has been seen in "Canzon: The Spear"; and the beloved in this poem is viewed in the same way:

And I have seen my Lady in the sun,
Her hair was spread about, a sheaf of wings,
And red the sunlight was, behind it all.

The speaker in the poem also becomes a transparent medium, defined solely by the love he bears for his lady:

Here am I come perforce my love of her,
Behold mine adoration
Maketh me clear . . .

By reacting upon her soul (Psyche), his love (Cupid) transcends all temporal limitations:

. . . and there are powers in this
Which, played on by the virtues of her soul,
Break down the four-square walls of standing time.

Thus the poem shows the union of Cupid and Psyche, in terms taken from Pater's retelling of that legend.

92

A poem that complements this vision very well is "Apparuit," published less than a year later. The title refers to Dante's description of his first seeing Beatrice, recorded in the *Vita Nuova*: "At that moment the animate spirit, which dwelleth in the lofty chamber whither all the senses carry their perceptions, was filled with wonder, and speaking more especially unto the spirits of the eyes, said these words: *Apparuit iam beatitudo vestra* [Your beatitude hath now been made manifest unto you] . . . I say that, from that time forward, Love quite governed my soul. . . ."[15] Pound was greatly attracted to the *Vita Nuova* for personal reasons, as he made clear in *The Spirit of Romance*: "That the *Vita Nuova* is the idealization of a real woman can be doubted by no one who has, even in the least degree, that sort of intelligence whereby it was written, or who has known in any degree the passion whereof it treats" (*SR*, 126). "Apparuit" is the "idealization of a real woman" who, although "a slight thing," becomes transformed into a radiant object of beauty, like the lady of "The House of Splendour":

> Golden rose the house, in the portal I saw
> thee, a marvel, carven in subtle stuff, a
> portent. Life died down in the lamp and flickered,
>   caught at the wonder.
>
> Crimson, frosty with dew, the roses bend where
> thou afar, moving in the glamorous sun,
> drinkst in life of earth, of the air, the tissue
>   golden about thee . . .   (*P*, 68)

Both these poems present the vision in explicitly medieval terms, here with images borrowed from Daniel and Ca-

[15] Dante Gabriel Rossetti, *Poems and Translations: 1850-1870* (London, 1926), p. 326.

valcanti. In the next poem in this series, "The Flame," this medieval vision of love is confronted by the modern world.

In "The Flame," Pound develops his definition of mystic love through the juxtaposition of a number of negative and affirmative statements. It is not something bound by conventions ("mates and mating") or the exchange of material objects:

> We who are wise beyond your dream of wisdom,
> Drink our immortal moments; we "pass through."
> We have gone forth beyond your bonds and borders,
> Provence knew;
> And all the tales of Oisin say but this:
> That men doth pass the net of days and hours.
>
> (P, 50)

These affirmations are recapitulations of positions already developed in "Canzoniere." The ecstatic experience can be only momentary; thus the highpoints of one's life are one or more "immortal moments," such as the moment that sustains Peire Vidal. This love also permits one to transcend space, to "pass through," like the speaker of "Canzon: The Spear." The reference to the "tales . . . of Oisin" connects Pound with the revival of Celtic legends by Yeats, and also with "The House of Splendour." In writing of the Cupid and Psyche legend in *The Spirit of Romance*, Pound has stated that "the probable allegory of the tale [of Cupid and Psyche], with a reversal of sex, is the same as that in the tales of Ywain and Ossian" (SR, 17). Oisin, through his relationship with Niamh, a goddess, succeeds in transcending time and space. Pound has always connected the pagan and mystic

94

aspects of Provence with the Celts: thus, a poem in *A Lume Spento* (reprinted in *Canzoni*) that concerns King Arthur's castle is given a Provençal title, "Li Bel Chasteus." Like the love of Oisin for Niamh, Pound's love transcends time as well as space ("doth pass the net of days and hours"), a notion developed in the preceding poem, where we saw love "break down the four-square walls of standing time."

In another context George Dekker has discussed the "relationship between Eros and Knowledge, between the flame and the light"[16] in Pound's work, and certainly this relationship is important in "The Flame." Dekker quotes a paragraph from "Psychology and Troubadours" which is relevant here: "Sex is, that is to say, of a double function and purpose, reproductive and educational; or, as we see in the realm of fluid force, one sort of vibration produces at different intensities, heat and light. No scientist would be so stupid as to affirm that heat produced light, and it is into a similar sort of false ratiocination that those writers fall who find the source of illumination, or of religious experience, centered solely in the philo-progenitive instinct" (*SR*, 94). In the lines that follow Pound relates these mystic moments of passion, which make one immortal, to the light of knowledge:

> We of the Ever-living, in that light
> Meet through our veils and whisper, and of love.
>
> (*P*, 50)

Not only does *fin' amors* transcend time, but those possessed by it are rendered immortal ("Ever-living"). This love also takes on the aspect of a secret cult ("We . . .

---

[16] George Dekker, *Sailing After Knowledge: The Cantos of Ezra Pound* (London, 1963), p. 46.

meet through our veils"), like that described in "Psychology and Troubadours."

In the next section, the relationship between Eros or Cupid and Knowledge is clarified. Again a series of negations is presented, which connect this poem with the first six in the series. Pound repeats those he had first mentioned, and continues by contrasting the temporal love of the nineties (with a reference to Arthur Symons)[17] with the permanent, immortal nature of *fin' amors*:

> There *is* the subtler music, the clear light
> Where time burns back about th' eternal embers.
> We are not shut from all the thousand heavens:
> Lo, there are many gods whom we have seen,
> Folk of unearthly fashion, places splendid,
> Bulwarks of beryl and of chrysophrase.   (*P*, 50)

The nature of the music Pound refers to here is clarified by a remark he made to Robert Fitzgerald, when the latter was visiting him at Rapallo: "I live in music for days at a time." Fitzgerald comments that "he did not mean the wordless music of the composers—Vivaldi, Antheil —who then interested him, but the music within himself, a visionary music requiring words."[18] Herbert Schneidau has noted that this might explain a statement made by Pound in a letter to Margaret Anderson in 1918: "I desire to go on with my long poem; and like the Duke of Chang, I desire to hear the music of a lost dynasty. (Have managed to hear it, in fact.)"[19] This "music" is clearly a sort of visionary knowledge, as indicated by its equation

[17] Noted in De Nagy, *The Poetry of Ezra Pound*, p. 41.

[18] Quoted in Herbert N. Schneidau, *Ezra Pound: The Image and the Real* (Baton Rouge, 1969), p. 144. Also in Norman, *Ezra Pound*, p. 310.

[19] *Ibid.*

with "the clear light / Where time burns back about th'
eternal embers." The sexual experience symbolized by
the "flame" is apparently a prelude to visionary knowl-
edge. This knowledge permits one to converse with the
gods, and to visit "places splendid," such as "The House
of Splendour."

Yet these visionary places are not all as remote from
our everyday experience as "The House of Splendour."
One such place is Benacus, the Latin name for the Lago
di Garda in Northern Italy:

> Sapphire Benacus, in thy mists and thee
> Nature herself's turned metaphysical,
> Who can look on that blue and not believe?   (*P*, 50)

It is not only a place of great beauty, but, as another
Canzoni poem indicates, it symbolizes the warm Medi-
terranean world:

> What hast thou, O my soul, with paradise?
> Will we not rather, when our freedom's won,
> Get us to some clear place wherein the sun
> Lets drift in on us through the olive leaves
> A liquid glory?   (*P*, 39)

Witemeyer, who has noted the connection between
" 'Blandula, Tenulla, Vagula' "[20] (cited above) and "The
Flame," has also pointed out the literary associations of
Garda for Pound: "Garda is a favorite, almost magical,
setting throughout Pound's poetry, hallowed by its as-
sociations with Catullus and with the Renaissance Latin
poet . . . Marc Antony Flaminius. It is a recurrent set-
ting in *The Cantos*, especially in the Pisan sequence, and

---

[20] The title is also from Pater, *Marius the Epicurean*, Vol.
I, p. 123. See Witemeyer, *The Poetry of Ezra Pound*, p. 99.

TOWARDS AN EMPYREAN OF PURE LIGHT

was the site of Pound's first meeting with Joyce."[21] So
great is the beauty of Benacus, that "Nature herself's
turned metaphysical." In " 'Blandula, Tenulla, Vagula' "
Pound describes the result of this beauty upon the recep-
tive beholder:

> If at Sirmio,
> My soul, I meet thee, when this life's outrun,
> Will we not find some headland consecrated
> By aery apostles of terrene delight,
> Will not our cult be founded on the waves,
> Clear sapphire, cobalt, cyanine,
> On triune azures, the impalpable
> Mirrors unstill of the eternal change?   (*P*, 39)

The final stanza of "The Flame" depicts the union
that the speaker has achieved with the blue purity of this
lake:

> If I have merged my soul, or utterly
> Am solved and bound in, through aught here
>   on earth,
> There canst thou find me, O thou anxious thou,
> Who call'st about my gates for some lost me;
> I say my soul flowed back, became translucent.
> Search not my lips, O Love, let go my hands,
> This thing that moves as man is no more mortal.
> If thou hast seen my shade sans character,
> If thou hast seen that mirror of all moments,
> That glass to all things that o'ershadow it,
> Call not that mirror me, for I have slipped
> Your grasp, I have eluded.   (*P*, 51)

It is the union of love (*fin' amors*) and the soul, or Cupid

[21] Witemeyer, *The Poetry of Ezra Pound*, p. 99.

98

and Psyche, that transcends all earthly bonds and achieves immortality.

One of the "immortal moments" mentioned in "The Flame" is presented in the next poem in the series, "Horae Beatae Inscriptio" ("an inscription for an hour of happiness"):

> How will this beauty, when I am far hence,
> Sweep back upon me and engulf my mind!
>
> How will these hours, when we twain are gray,
> Turned in their sapphire tide, come flooding o'er us!
>
> (P, 51)

Here the speaker projects an experience in which the ideal has become realized through space and time, thereby affirming its immortality. The type of epiphany referred to here is similar to that described in "Erat Hora," a *Canzoni* poem with a more contemporary setting:

> "Thank you, whatever comes." And then she
>   turned
> And, as the ray of sun on hanging flowers
> Fades when the wind hath lifted them aside,
> Went swiftly from me. Nay, whatever comes
> One hour was sunlit and the most high gods
> May not make boast of any better thing
> Than to have watched that hour as it passed. (P, 40)

These moments of ecstasy are the basis for divine illumination and thus constitute the most important experience in Pound's world.

The milieu in which the modern artist functions, and the conventions by which he regulates his life, are presented in "Au Salon." He has exchanged "li bel chasteus" for "le salon," but he continues to write for a select few:

> Some circle of not more than three
> > that we prefer to play up to,
> Some few whom we'd rather please
> > than hear the whole aegrum vulgus
> Splitting its beery jowl
> > a-meaowling our praises.
>
> (P, 52)

Gods, too, the contemporary poet must have, so for the everyday tasks of the modern world he invokes the household gods which, according to Pater (who mentions them on the opening page of *Marius the Epicurean*) represent "the older and purer forms of Paganism."[22] And while his songs may no longer move kingdoms, their contribution to society is no less great: "sic crescit gloria mundi" ("thus the glory of the world increases").

Thus, although the contours of his world have changed radically, the poet continues to maintain certain traditions and goals that remain valid after many centuries.

The final poem in the series, "Au Jardin," considers the relationship between the poet and the lady he is praising. As Witemeyer has noted, the poem is a riposte to Yeats's "The Cap and the Bells."[23] In Yeats's poem, the jester first gives his heart and soul to the lady and, failing to gain her attention, finally presents her with his cap and bells —a rather clear phallic image. Pound's poet does not accept Yeats's conclusion ("I will send them to her and die"); his association with his lady will be quite different:

> Well, there's no use your loving me
> That way, Lady;
> For I've nothing but songs to give you.   (P, 53)

[22] Pater, *Marius the Epicurean*, Vol. i, p. 3.
[23] See Witemeyer, *The Poetry of Ezra Pound*, p. 101.

Pound's persona desires more than the *fals' amors* of Yeats's jester, which is obviously not productive.

The speaker in "Au Jardin" is one in a long line of personae beginning with "Cino" and "Marvoil" who are concerned with the problem of the relationship between the poet and his patron, or, more generally, his public. The speaker here is clearly a medieval troubadour whose language, in fact, echos Daniel's:

> I am set wide upon the world's ways
> To say that life is, some way, a gay thing . . .
>
> [Bona es vida pos joia la mante . . .]

He affirms life in the most colloquial terms and states unequivocally that he is not interested in the type of relationship Yeats's jester had with his lady, but rather desires one that will transcend mere sexuality.

In his search for values with which he can confront the chaos of the contemporary world, Pound has retraced his steps through Tuscany to Provence. In the medieval world stretching from the Troubadours to Dante, Pound finds a civilization whose ideals appeal greatly to him. He outlines the contours of this radiant world in the "Canzoniere" sequence first published in *Provença*, and in "Und Drang" he shows the importance of these values for the modern world. His further work in medievalism, throughout *The Cantos* and in his studies of "Donna mi prega," merely builds upon the conclusions he had reached by 1912: this world will become the basis of his "ultimate heaven . . . [his] Empyrean of pure light" (*SR*, 151).

Chapter IV

EXERCISES IN THE MOTHER TONGUE:
Versions of Daniel

The Twelfth Century, or, more exactly, that century whose center is the year 1200, has left us two perfect gifts: the church of San Zeno in Verona, and the canzoni of Arnaut Daniel.

The Spirit of Romance

And there is no high-road to the Muses.

Homage to Sextus Propertius

AMONG the Provençal poets in Pound's work, Arnaut Daniel occupies a singular position. Pound has never considered his personality interesting enough to be utilized as a persona: indeed, in all of Pound's many writings about Daniel (including Pound's imitation *razo*) there is only one mention of Daniel as a living individual; this is unusual in terms of the interest Pound has taken in the lives of the troubadours. In writing of "Can chai la fueilla," Pound has stated: "This [poem] comes from a very real, very much alive young man who has kicked over the traces, told his instructors to go to hell, put his title 'En' ('Sir') in his wallet, and set out to see life as a jongleur."[1]

[1] Pound, "Osiris, v," *New Age*, x, 9 (Dec. 28, 1911), p. 201.

Although there is material here for a poem, Pound never developed it as he did the *vidas* of other Provençal poets. Daniel has remained for him quite simply "the finest of the troubadours": "I do not mean by that that he has written anything more poignant than de Born's 'Si tuit li dol el plor el marrimen,' or anything more haunting than Vidal's 'Ab l'alen tir vas me l'aire,' or that his personality was more poetic than that of Arnaut de Marvoil, or his mind more subtle than that of Aimeric de Bellenoi; but simply that Arnaut's work as a whole is more interesting."[2] It is on Daniel's *work*—in its entirety—that Pound has concentrated. In none of his early volumes did he publish individual translations of Daniel's poems, although, as we have seen, he did use two of Daniel's forms: the sestina and the *canso*. Pound obviously felt that one must approach Daniel through his total *oeuvre*; this accounts for the allotment of an entire chapter to him in *The Spirit of Romance*. When Pound published translations of Daniel's work, first in "I Gather the Limbs of Osiris" and later in *Instigations* and *Umbra*, he presented over half of Daniel's poems, thus permitting the reader to approach Daniel's work in bulk.

Pound's concern with Daniel has been influenced to a large extent by Dante's estimation of his work. Dante cites several of Daniel's poems in *De Vulgari Eloquentia* (as we noticed in the preceding chapter) and also in the *Purgatorio*, where Daniel is referred to as "the better craftsman in the mother tongue." Daniel replies to this assertation in Provençal, thus being the only person in *The Divine Comedy* to have the honor of speaking in his own language. Pound quotes from Dante at great length in the chapter on Daniel in *The Spirit of Romance*, and

[2] Pound, "Osiris, xi," *New Age*, x, 16 (Feb. 15, 1912), p. 370.

it is obvious that Dante's appreciation of Daniel is the source of Pound's interest in him.

Pound's initial concern with Daniel was due to his technical virtuosity and "craftsmanship." Indeed, Pound has ranked him among the "inventors," a very small group of artists who are "discoverers of a particular process or of more than one mode and process. Sometimes," Pound continues, "these people are known, or discoverable; for example, we know, with reasonable certitude, that Arnaut Daniel introduced certain methods of rhyming, and we know that certain finenesses of perception appeared first in such a troubadour or in G. Cavalcanti" (*LE*, 23:1929). An artist must be aware of the discoveries of these "inventors" if he is to avoid the onerous drudgery of repeating their work: "The experimental demonstrations of one man may save the time of many—hence my furore over Arnaut Daniel—if a man's experiments try out one new rime, or dispense conclusively with one iota of currently accepted nonsense, he is merely playing fair with his colleagues when he chalks up his result" (*LE*, 10:1912).

What, then, were these stylistic innovations? Pound catalogued them in some detail in an article preceding his first poetic translations of Daniel in "I Gather the Limbs of Osiris":

"Now in the flower of this age, when many people were writing canzoni . . . Arnaut discriminated between rhyme and rhyme.

"He perceived, that is, that the beauty to be gotten from a similarity of line-terminations depends not upon their multiplicity, but upon their action the one upon the other; not upon frequency, but upon the manner of sequence and combination. . . . Arnaut uses what for want of a better term I call polyphonic rhyme.

"At a time when both prose and poetry were loose-jointed, prolix, barbaric, he, to all intents and virtually, rediscovered 'style.' He conceived, that is, a manner of writing in which each word should bear some burden, should make some special contribution to the effect of the whole. The poem is an organism in which each part functionates [sic], gives to sound or to sense something —preferably to sound *and* sense gives something.

"Thirdly, he discerns what Plato had discerned some time before, that μέλος is the union of words, rhythm, and music (i.e., that part of music which we do not perceive as rhythm). Intense hunger for a strict accord between these three has marked only the best lyric periods, and Arnaut felt this hunger more keenly and more precisely than his fellows or his forerunners.

"He is significant for all these things. He bears to the technique of *accented* verse of Europe very much the same relation that Euclid does to our mathematics. . . ."[3]

Daniel is praised for his "polyphonic rhyme," based on his realization that "The music of rhymes depends upon their arrangement, not on their multiplicity."[4] Kenner calls this a "polyphony, not of simultaneous elements which are impossible in poetry, but of something chiming from something we remember from earlier, earlier in . . . [the] poem and out of earlier poems."[5] It is similar to the principle of repetition we noticed in "Na Audiart" and

[3] Pound, "Osiris, IV," *New Age*, x, 8 (Dec. 21, 1911), p. 179.
[4] Pound, *The Spirit of Romance*, p. 38. In the same work (p. 50), Pound makes a similar observation with regard to Yeats: "Yeats gives me to understand that there comes a time in the career of a great poet when he ceases to take pleasure in riming 'mountain' with 'fountain' and 'beauty' with 'duty.' "
[5] Hugh Kenner, "Horizontal Chords," *Sumac*, II (Winter/Spring 1970), p. 227.

"Near Perigord," and it later becomes a principle of organization in *The Cantos*, where "structural analogies, reinforced by rhythm, do the work of assertion."[6]

He is also praised for developing two types of writing that Pound classifies elsewhere as "melopoeia" and "logopoeia." He has defined "melopoeia" as a "kind of poetry . . . wherein the words are charged, over and above their plain meaning, with some musical property, which directs the bearing or trend of that meaning" (*LE*, 25: 1929). Provençal poetry, where the music and words were equally important, presents possibilities for "melopoeia" not always to be found in poetry composed on a typewriter. "It is mainly for the sake of the melopoeia that one investigates troubadour poetry" (*ABC*, 52), Pound states in *ABC of Reading* (1934), where he also notes that "poetry begins to atrophy when it gets too far from music" (*ABC*, 14).

The second type of writing, "logopoeia," is defined by Pound as " 'the dance of the intellect among words,' that is to say, it employs words not only for their direct meaning, but it takes count in a special way of habits of usage, of the context we *expect* to find with the word, its usual concomitants, of its known acceptances, and of ironical play" (*LE*, 25:1929). Daniel's "logopoeia" can be seen in his search for *le mot juste*, resulting in his precision of language, "that explicit rendering, be it of external nature, or of emotion" (*LE*, 11:1912) that Pound also praises in Dante and Cavalcanti. This precision creates problems for the lazy reader, as Pound notes in explaining the difficulty of reading Daniel: This difficulty "is due not so much to obscurities of style, or to such as are caused by the constraints of complicated form, and

[6] *Ibid.*, p. 230.

exigency of scarce rimes, but mainly to his refusal to use the 'journalese' of his day, and to his aversion from an obvious familiar vocabulary" (*SR*, 25). Daniel (whose example Pound follows) was concerned with revitalizing his own language: "And En Arnaut was the best artist among the Provençals, trying the speech in new fashions, and bringing new words into writing, and making new blendings of words" (*LE*, 111:1920).

A third type of writing, not mentioned in the passage from "I Gather the Limbs of Osiris" cited above, but none the less important in any discussion of Daniel's work, is "phanopoeia." Pound defines "phanopoeia" as "a casting of images upon the visual imagination" (*LE*, 25:1929). In Daniel's work there are a number of images to which Pound has ascribed a "visionary significance," images such as the "fair mantle of indigo" and "the glamor of the lamplight" in "Doutz brais e critz." It is partly upon examples of "phanopoeia" such as these that Pound developed the mystical interpretation of Provençal poetry considered in the previous chapter.

These, then, are the reasons for which Pound values the work of Daniel so greatly. In Daniel's poems he finds the precision of language he so admires in Dante, the introduction of a number of new stanzaic forms, a brilliant use of rhyme, and a thorough development of "melopoeia," "phanopoeia," and "logopoeia." Pound attempts to retain these qualities in his translations of Daniel, which we will consider next.

In Chapter 1, we concluded that Pound's most persistent problems with the early translations were in creating an English equivalent for the Provençal and in finding an appropriate form into which to translate these poems. The early translations undoubtedly constituted an important series of technical exercises for Pound, as they forced him to stretch the resources of English to accommodate his material, in addition to being a "series of masks" for him. In these translations Pound rarely employed the Provençal stanza forms without some modification: in fact, his first use of the *coblas unissonans* was in the series of *cansos* published in "Canzoniere," which, of course, preceded his metrical translations of Daniel. Pound's first translations of Daniel (in *The Spirit of Romance*) are mostly in prose. Of his second group of translations (in "I Gather the Limbs of Osiris"), ten are in poetry and one in prose; *Hesternae Rosae* contains two poetic translations; and in *Instigations* and *Umbra* there are poetic translations of ten poems. Some of the poems are translated as many as three times, with each translation being quite different from the previous versions. By considering Pound's treatment of several of Daniel's poems over a period of years, we can gain some idea of how he develops as a translator, and the extent to which he overcomes the problems of his earlier translations.

"Sols sui qui sai lo sobrafan quem sortz" is one of Daniel's poems that has most occupied Pound; the different attempts he has made to translate this poem are indicative of his work with Daniel as a whole. In *The Spirit of Romance*, Pound published a verse translation of stanza 1, accompanied by a prose translation of the entire poem. The prose is by and large a literal translation:

> Sols sui qui sai lo sobrafan quem sortz
> Al cor d'amor sofren per sobramar,
> Car mos volers es tant ferms et entiers
> C'anc no s'esduis de celliei ni s'estors
> Cui encubic al prim vezer e puois:

Qu'ades ses lieis dic a lieis cochos motz,
Pois quan la vei non sai, tant l'ai, que dire.[7]

    I am the only one who knows the over-anguish
which falls to my lot, to the heart of love suffering
through over-love; for my desire is so firm and whole,
never turning away or twisting from her, whom I de-
sired at first sight and since, so that now without her
I say to her hot words, since when I see her I do not
know, having so much, what to say.   (*SR*, 27)

"Over-anguish" and "over-love" are accurate renditions
of the Provençal "sobrafan" and "sobramor," but this
type of compound is much less effective in English.
Pound's translation of "cochos" ("eager") as "hot" is an
attempt to suggest the poet's passion, but the expression
is rather trite in this context. In general, the translation is
rather inert. There are some changes in the accompany-
ing poetic version, which make it a more interesting and
less ponderous rendition:

Only I know what over-anguish falls
Upon the love-worn heart through over-love.
Because of my desire so firm and whole
Toward her I loved on sight and since alway,
Which turneth not aside nor wavereth.
So, far from her, I speak for her mad speech,
Who near her, for o'er much to speak, am dumb.
         (*SR*, 26)

[7] Text in *La Vita e le Opere del Trovatore Arnaldo Daniello*,
ed. U. A. Canello (Halle, 1883), p. 115. Reprinted in *The Trans-
lations of Ezra Pound* (p. 178). This was the standard text until
the edition of R. Lavaud (Toulouse, 1910), which Pound re-
ferred to for his final versions of Daniel.

Although the language here is more compressed, Pound effortlessly lapses into the Pre-Raphaelite diction that, as we noted, permeates his early work. Expressions like "love-worn heart," "since alway," and "o'er much" betray him at once. He is very slow to liberate himself from this influence. However, in "I Gather the Limbs of Osiris" he makes an extremely important step in this direction by distinguishing between Daniel's medievalism and that of the Pre-Raphaelites:

". . . You will note that they [i.e., his translations of Daniel] are all free from what Morris and Rossetti—and the smaragdite poets generally—have taught us to regard as mediaevalism, and that they undoubtedly contain many a turn which would have delighted Robert Browning. . . .

"I do not mean to assail *plat ventre* the mediaevalism of the Victorian mediaevalists. Their mediaevalism was that of the romances of North France, of magical ships, and the rest of it, of Avalons that were not; a very charming mediaevalism if you like it—I do more or less—but there is also the mediaevalism of mediaeval life as it was.

> 'Bona es vida
>
>   pos joia la mante,'

bawls Arnaut in 'Can chai la fueilla.' 'Bully is living where joy can back it up.' This comes from a very real, very much alive young man who . . . will see no stags with crosses growing from their foreheads, he will not fly to an imprisoned lady in the form of a hawk; he will, I think, preserve through life a pleasing sense of humor. . . ."[8]

Here Pound recognizes the limitations and inaccuracies

[8] Pound, "Osiris, v," *New Age*, x, 9 (Dec. 28, 1911), p. 201.

of the medievalism of the Pre-Raphaelites, whose themes and language are more representative of Victorian England than anything truly medieval. Pound thus associates himself with a world view closer to Browning than Rossetti and Morris, although traces of their language certainly linger here. It is interesting to note, with regard to what Pound says above, that Francis Hueffer referred to Daniel as "the Browning of Provençal literature" in his study of the troubadours, although primarily for stylistic reasons.[9] In the translation of "Sols sui," published in "I Gather the Limbs of Osiris," there are traces of both Browning and Rossetti:

> Only I know what over-anguish falls
> Upon the heart of love so over-borne,
> My over-longing that's so whole and strong
> Turns not from her, nay never since these eyes
> First saw her has the flame upon them quailed.
> And I, afar, speak to her words like flame,
> And near her, having much, there's nought for saying.[10]

Pound retains the first line of the earlier version, but makes some interesting changes in the second. He drops the rather banal "love-worn heart," and retranslates "over-love" ("sobramar") as "over-longing," substituting it for "desire" in line 3. He creates a new compound word ("over-borne") which is an improvement upon "love-worn heart," although the result is an excess of compounds beginning with "over." By rearranging lines 3-5 somewhat in the new version, Pound has created a more natural word order. He has also introduced the concept

[9] Hueffer, *The Troubadours*, p. 48.
[10] Pound, "Osiris, xii," *New Age*, x, 17 (Feb. 22, 1912), p. 392.

111

of "flame" (replacing "hot words"), which we have seen before in his translation of "Dompna Pois" ("such flame-lap") and in "The Flame"; and this is a much better expression of the passion that lies behind his reticence. This rendition is more interpretative than the earlier one. Moreover, Pound has maintained the rhyme scheme of the original throughout the entire poem. Thus the second stanza reads:

> To others blind I am, deaf to their calls;
> In solely her, sight, sound and wonder are born.
> In all this speech I do the truth no wrong,
> Yet my mouth cannot speak the heart's device;
> Hills, dales, roads, plains! O'er all these were I haled
> I'd find in no one form such charms to fame
> As God hath set in her for their assaying.[11]

At the time Pound was working on these translations in "I Gather the Limbs of Osiris," it was his intention to publish them as a separate edition of Daniel's poems, similar to his edition of Cavalcanti. In August 1912 he wrote to Harriet Monroe that he had sent *"Arnaut Daniel . . .* to the publisher" (*L*, 9). Pound was sufficiently optimistic to include *The Canzoni of Arnaut Daniel*, R. F. Seymour & Co., Chicago in a bibliographical note that appeared in *Des Imagistes* (1914). Seymour, however, was not interested in Pound's work. As he later explained to Charles Norman: "I had a manuscript in this office for a year or more, returning it only because my then partner thought Pound bad business. It was a translation of a jongleur's chanson, and Walter Morse Rummel had tran-

[11] *Ibid.*

112

scribed the funny-looking musical notation into what I supposed was trustworthy modern notation."[12] At some point the manuscript was lost, and thus this edition never appeared. In retrospect, Pound considered this a good thing. In 1918 he wrote to Harriet Monroe: "I am profoundly glad my earlier versions of Arnaut weren't published. It gives me a chance to do something with it" (*L*, 127). This "something" was the series of translations finally published in *Instigations* (1920).

By 1917 Pound was retranslating Daniel, and the outcome is quite different from his early efforts. "Is a fine poet ever translated until another his equal invents a new style in a later language," Pound asks in "Notes on Elizabethan Classicists" (*LE*, 235: 1917-1918). These translations provide an answer, for at last he has found what he feels to be an English equivalent of Provençal. "Sols sui," the first of these poems to be republished (it appeared as the last poem in the sequence "Homage à la Langue d'Oc," 1918), illustrates this language well:

I only, and who elrische pain support
Know out love's heart o'er borne by overlove,
For my desire that is so firm and straight
And unchanged since I found her in my sight
And unturned since she came within my glance,
That far from her my speech springs up aflame;
Near her comes not. So press the words to arrest it.

I am blind to others, and their retort
I hear not. In her alone, I see, move,
Wonder . . . And jest not. And the words dilate
Not truth; but mouth speaks not the heart outright;

> I could not walk roads, flats, dales, hills, by chance,
> To find charm's sum within one single frame
> As God hath set in her t'assay and test it.   (*T*, 179)

There is a vigor and strength here that the other versions lack. This can easily be seen by comparing a line from all four versions (stanza 1, line 6):

> So that now without her I say to her hot words (1910)
> So, far from her, I speak for her mad speech (1910)
> And I, afar, speak to her words like flame (1912)
> That far from her my speech springs up aflame (1917)

With one exception, the image is the same, and yet the movement of the last line is far more forceful and direct than any of the earlier versions.

The language remains archaic, and yet the antiquated terms that strike one here ("elrische," "Gentrice," "prate," "paregale," "galzeardy," and "lyt") are very different from the archaisms of the 1910 and 1912 versions. These archaisms reflect Pound's extensive reading of the Elizabethan and pre-Elizabethan translators whose work he discusses in "Notes on Elizabethan Classicists" (1917-1918). For Pound the most important of these is Gavin Douglas, "a great poet" (*LE*, 247). He quotes at length from Douglas' translation of the *Aeneis* both here and in *ABC of Reading*, and draws extensively upon Douglas' diction in these translations. Pound has banished Morris and Rossetti and has *created* a language that, in his mind, successfully reproduces the Provençal sensibility. This language is archaic, because the feelings being expressed are archaic, but it is a new language, totally unlike that of the Pre-Raphaelites.

The quality of this new language can best be felt by considering still another example, Pound's translations of "Doutz brais e critz." In the preceding chapter we noticed the importance of this poem for Pound, especially the "visionary" third and fourth stanzas, the last line of which Pound has often quoted as a singular mark of Daniel's excellence.[18] Let us consider his versions of these two stanzas. In Provençal they read:

> Ben fui grazitz
> E mas paraulas coutas,
> Per so que jes al chausir no fui pecs,
> Anz volgui mais prendre fin aur que ram,
> Lo jorn quez ieu e midonz nos baizem
> Em fetz escut de son bel mantel endi
> Que lausengier fals, lenga de colobra,
> Non o visson, don tan mals motz escampa.
>
> Dieus lo chauzitz,
> Per cui foron assoutas
> Las faillidas que fetz Longis lo cecs,
> Voilla, sil platz, qu'ieu e midonz jassam
> En la chambra on amdui nos mandem
> Uns rics convens don tan gran joi atendi,
> Quel seu bel cors baisan rizen descobra
> E quel remir contral lum de la lampa.   (T, 172, 174)

Pound has translated this quite literally in *The Spirit of Romance*, although his language is not without touches of the Pre-Raphaelites:

"Well was I welcomed and my words attended, so that I was not wrong in choosing her, but I wished rather to

[18] This line "may be taken to differentiate Arnaut Daniel from all other poets of Provence" (*SR*, 34).

take the gold than a twig, that day when I and my lady kissed, and she made me a shield of her fair dark blue mantle, so that the false tale-bearers should not see us; the tale-bearers with their cobra's tongues, whence so many ill words are set abroad.

"May God, the Chosen, by whom were absolved the sins of the blind Longinus, wish if it please him, that I and my lady lie within one chamber where we shall make a rich covenant, whereon great joy attendeth; where, with laughter and caresses, she shall disclose to me her fair body, with the glamor of the lamplight about it" (*SR*, 34).

The rendition of this in "I Gather the Limbs of Osiris" represents, as with the corresponding translation of "Sols sui," a sort of transitional stage between Pre-Raphaelite medievalism and Pound's own medievalism:

> With clear replies,
>   And my talk undisputed,
> I was received. And nothing can impeach
> My choice of her. Good gold I got in fee,
> Not copper, when we kissed at that day's end.
> And she made over me a shield, extending
> Her mantle of indigo, fair, to th' excision
> Of liars' sight, who've serpents' tongues perfected.
>
> God who did'st rise,
>   And by whom were commuted
> Longinus his blind sin, Thee I beseech
> That we lie in some room communally
> And seal that pact whereon such joys attend.
> There with embraces and low laughter blending

Until she give her body to my vision,
There with the glamour of the lamp reflected.[14]

One is struck in reading this version (or singing it, as Pound would have us do) that it is more straightforward than the prose translation. There are a few minor changes, principally in the opening of the second stanza, and, if anything, the meaning is clearer here. Some of the language is stilted: "Until she give her body to my vision" is a rather static phrase, not nearly as descriptive as Daniel's. "Impeach" is a poor choice of verb, obviously selected for its rhyme, as is "excision." But generally the language (even with the strict restrictions of this stanza form) is clearer and more descriptive than the prose version.

The final translation of this poem, published in *Instigations*, has an entirely different tone and movement, at once more colloquial and yet more antiquated:

Welcome not lax,
                      and my words were protected
Not blabbed to other, when I set my likes
On her. Not brass but gold was 'neath the die.
That day we kissed, and after it she flacked
O'er me her cloak of indigo, for screening
Me from all culvertz' eyes, whose blathered bluster
Can set such spites abroad; win jibes for wages.

God who did tax
                      not Longus' sin, respected
That blind centurion beneath the spikes
And him forgave, grant that we two shall lie
Within one room, and seal therein our pact,

---

[14] Pound, "Osiris, xii," *New Age*, x (Feb. 22, 1912), p. 393.

117

Yes, that she kiss me in the half-light, leaning
To me, and laugh and strip and stand forth in the lustre
Where lamp-light with light limb but half engages.

(*T*, 173, 175)

Pound has not only changed the diction entirely here, but some of the images as well: thus the image in the third line of the first stanza, which in the earlier version applied to the kissing ("Good gold I got in fee / Not copper, when we kissed") is now applied directly to the lady. He has also elaborated at length upon the illusion to Longinus, thus making the invocation to God all the more forceful. As Kenner has stated: "This isn't 'Ah God,' but the God who on a specific occasion forgave Longinus and granted him sight: on the occasion, moreover, when Longinus had run his spear into the side of God incarnate. Sins augment the wounds of Christ; Arnaut boldly proposes a sin that shall culminate, like Longinus', in vision: and the light, and the paradisal *tan gran joi*, help lend her lovely body, *seu bel cors*, the force of 'Hoc est corpus,' a revealed miracle, to adore."[15] The colloquial tone creates a much greater vividness, especially in the last three lines of the second stanza, where the woman's sexuality is made very appealing. Here she becomes a passionate woman, and yet Pound manages to retain the softness and warmth that Daniel's final line communicates.

In the series of translations published in *Instigations*, two of which we have examined here, Pound succeeds in developing a language for Provençal, as well as in translating difficult *canso* forms into English. The technical virtuosity we have witnessed is considerable, but the ultimate success of these translations, as English poems,

[15] Kenner, "Horizontal Chords," p. 229.

is questionable. Pound was well aware of this. In 1922, he wrote to Felix Schelling:

"My assults on Provence: 1st: using it as subject matter, trying to do as R. B. had with Renaissance Italy. 2, Diagrammatic translations (those of Arnaut, now printed in *Instigations*); all part of study of verse-form (as trans. of Cavalcanti). Note that the English 'poet' en masse had simply said: 'these forms are *impossible* in English, they are too complicated, we haven't the rhymes.' That was bunkum, usual laziness of English, and hatred of craft. (I suppose I have by now a right to be serious about this matter, having been plugging at it for twenty years.) Eh bien. 1. I have proved that the Provençal rhyme schemes are not *impos*sible in English. They are probably *inadvis*able. The troubadour was not worried by our sense of style, our 'literary values,' he could shovel in words in any order he liked. Milton ruined his work by not understanding that the genius of English is not the genius of Latin, and that one can NOT write an uninflected language in the same way, using the same word-order that serves in an inflected language. The troubadour, fortunately perhaps, was not worried about English order; he got certain musical effects because he cd. concentrate on music without bothering about literary values. He had a kind of freedom which we no longer have" (*L*, 179). There is, of course, much more to these translations than merely a study of verse forms, just as Pound learned more from Cavalcanti than he indicates above. Quite apart from the many qualities in Daniel that Pound admired, qualities that influenced both Pound's art and his conception of the artist, Pound created—through his work on Daniel's poems—an English version of Provençal. Pound's early translations fail largely because all too often they are translated into the idiom of

119

the time. Pound gradually learned that the translator, like
the birds in Daniel's *canso* "Autet e bas," must sing "en
son us," in his own voice. For each foreign poet or tradi-
tion it became necessary to create a new language in Eng-
lish: thus, we find one language for the translations in
Cathay, another for "The Seafarer," and quite a different
one for the poems of Provence. The state of mind to
which this language corresponds is perhaps best illus-
trated by the sequence of poems entitled "Homage à la
Langue d'Oc," Pound's last systematic poetic approach
to Provençal culture, and the subject of the next chapter.

Chapter V

PROVENCE REVISITED:
"Homage à la Langue d'Oc"

Yet you ask on what account I write so many love-lyrics
And whence this soft book comes into my mouth.
Neither Calliope nor Apollo sung these things into my ear,
My genius is no more than a girl.
Homage to Sextus Propertius

"HOMAGE [sic] à la Langue d'Oc," as it was initially titled,[1] is Pound's last poetic treatment of Provence before *The Cantos*. It appeared twice in periodicals before being published in *Quia Pauper Amavi* (1919), where it was the first of four sequences, the other being "Moeurs Contemporains," "Three Cantos," and *Homage to Sextus Propertius*. It has received less consideration and acclaim than the other "homage" with which it was published, although the two works have much in common: both are "homages" to past cultures that, presumably, have some relevance for the present; both deal with the topic of

[1] Actually, it was first published as "Homage à la Langue d'Or," but this error was corrected with republication.

121

love, as the title of the volume suggests;[2] and the language in both is very important. It is quite obvious, from their titles and placement in this volume, that Pound intended them to be considered as a pair, and we might begin our examination of "Homage à la Langue d'Oc" by observing its similarities to *Homage to Sextus Propertius*.

In explaining what he meant by "homage," Pound cited the example of Debussy's "Hommage à Rameau," that is, "a piece of music recalling Rameau's manner."[3] There are obviously many ways to capture the "manner" of another author or culture; one of the means Pound employs in both works is translation. An equally important method is what he has called "excernement" (*LE*, 75), for both homages are highly selective in the material they present, and this selection is in itself a critical act. The musical analogy is interesting here, for one of the principal qualities of the "Homage à la Langue d'Oc" is, in Pound's opinion, its "music" (*L*, 179) and indeed the most successful poem in that sequence is the "Descant on a Theme by Cerclamon [sic]."[4]

The language of both sequences is extremely important, for this is one means by which Pound contrasts the sensibilities of Provence and Rome. In a letter to Felix E. Schelling, Pound has clarified this point: "The point of

[2] The title is taken from Ovid's *Ars Amatoria* (II, 165): "Pauperibus vates ego sum, quia pauper amavi" ("I am the poet of the poor, because I was poor when I loved"—Loeb), quoted in Ruthven, *A Guide to Ezra Pound's "Personae" (1926)*, p. 87.

[3] P. Hutchins, "Ezra Pound and Thomas Hardy," *Southern Review*, IV, 1 (Jan. 1968), p. 99. Quoted in *loc.cit.*

[4] Pound consistently misspells Cercamon's name, although he used the proper form in "Troubadours: Their Sorts and Conditions (1913)."

the archaic language in the Prov. trans. is that the Latin is really 'modern.' We are just getting back to a Roman state of civilization, or in reach of it; whereas the Provençal feeling is archaic, we are ages away from it. (Whether I have managed to convey this or not I can't say; but it is the reason for the archaic dialect.)" (*L*, 179.) In the previous chapter we saw Pound laboring to create a language for Provençal and finally developing one that was both archaic and colloquial. This is essentially the language he used in "Homage à la Langue d'Oc," although here one finds an even greater French influence, both in the vocabulary of individual poems (e.g., "venust," "plasmatour") and in some of the titles ("Homage à la Langue d'Oc" and "Avril"). The contrast between this diction and the modern language of *Homage to Sextus Propertius* emphasizes the difference in their treatment of love, which is significant. However, there are some similarities between the love ethic of Propertius and that of the troubadours, as J. P. Sullivan has noted in *Ezra Pound and Sextus Propertius*: "The similarities between Courtly Love and the Propertian attitude toward love are close. . . . The 'feudalization of love,' the humility of the lover, exemplified in the poets of the Languedoc, is paralleled by the *servitium amoris* of the Roman elegist; serf or slave, the human situation is the same. Even the adulterous nature of Courtly Love may be paralleled in the elegists. . . . Jealousy, of course, needs no dwelling upon, and the religion of Love that we see in Troubadour poetry is the lineal descendant . . . of the sort of poetry that Pound used for . . . [*Homage to Sextus Propertius*]."[5]

[5] J. P. Sullivan, *Ezra Pound and Sextus Propertius: A Study in Creative Translation* (Austin, 1964), pp. 51-52.

Pound was well aware of this similarity, as indicated by the frequency with which he quotes his favorite line from Propertius ("Ingenium nobis ipsa puella facit") in discussions of the troubadours. It symbolizes Pound's perception of the "relationship between sexual activity, artistic creation, and intellectual advancement"[6] that we noticed in Chapter III. But more important in this sequence is Pound's idealized treatment of the lady, which contrasts sharply with the ironic treatment in Propertius.

Finally, both of the cultures represented in these poems have values relevant to the modern age. We have already noted the position occupied by medieval values in Pound's cosmos, and Pound has said the same thing about Propertius' world: ". . . it [*Homage to Sextus Propertius*] presents certain emotions as vital to me in 1917, faced with the infinite and ineffable imbecility of the British Empire, as they were to Propertius some centuries earlier, when faced with the infinite and ineffable imbecility of the Roman Empire" (*L*, 231).

By publishing these two sequences together, Pound hoped to make their similarities clear to the reader, so that they would illuminate each other. T. S. Eliot, in an early review of this volume, noted this structure and stated that the work was "probably the most significant book that he [Pound] has published . . . [and] the most coherent extended work since 'Personae' and 'Exultations.' "[7]

"Homage à la Langue d'Oc" consists of six poems, three of which are *albas*. As we noted earlier, Pound's selection is a critical one, and the emphasis in this "hom-

---

[6] Ruthven, *A Guide to Ezra Pound's "Personae"* (*1926*), p. 105.

[7] T. S. Eliot, "The Method of Mr. Pound," *The Athenaeum*, 4,669 (Oct. 24, 1919), p. 1,065.

age" is clearly upon the Provençal tradition of love po-
etry: there are no examples of the *sirventes, planh,* or
tenso, and Bertran de Born, one of Pound's early favo-
rites, is conspicuous by his absence. The entire series deals
with love and its vicissitudes, and develops a consistent
interpretation of the effect of *Amor* on those it influ-
ences. There is a good deal of metrical freedom here, as
Pound experiments with stanzas of varying lengths. Al-
though three of the poems have been translated previ-
ously, all the versions are unique to this volume.

The opening poem is a brief *alba,* presented from the
point of view of the participant. Pound's rendition is ex-
tremely effective, and he manages to have even more
rhymes than the Provençal:

> Quan lo rossinhols escria
> ab sa par la nueg e·l dia,
> yeu suy ab ma bell' amia
>   ios la flor,
> tro la gaita de la tor
> escria: drutz, al leuar!
> qu'ieu vey l'alba e·l iorn clar.[8]

> When the nightingale to his mate
> Sings day-long and night late
> My love and I keep state
> In bower,
> In flower,
> 'Till the watchman on the tower
> Cry:
>   "Up! Thou rascal, Rise,
>   I see the white
>   Light

[8] Text in Appel, *Provenzalische Chrestomathie,* p. 90.

125

> And the night
> Flies."
>
> (P, 171)

As the opening poem, it presents an attitude toward love that establishes the tone of the sequence. Love is seen as transitory, impermanent, and, by implication at least, adulterous. Unlike the other two *albas* in the series, there is no one here but the lover to judge the situation, and the graceful movement and charm of this poem suggest that love is a delightful experience.

This *alba* also shows Pound's experimentation with line lengths and typography, something that he does to a much greater extent in the "Descant on a Theme by Cerclamon." Donald Davie has spoken of Pound's attempts "to explore more audaciously the resources modern typography provides for thus controlling very imperiously the tempo, the stops and starts, that the reader is to observe in his reading,"[9] and he traces this development to Pound's work with "Donna mi prega" (1932): "In Pound's case he was led to them [i.e., these mannerisms], not just by the availability of a typewriting machine, but by seeking to translate a poet of medieval Italy so scrupulously as to bring over even what that poet's speech sounded like in that poet's ear."[10] In the *alba* Pound is also reproducing the sound of the "poet's speech," and it should be noted that this poem precedes his translation of "Donna mi prega" by fourteen years.

The second poem in the sequence is another *alba*, this time seen from the point of view of the watchman, or at least a close friend who has assumed this role. As Wilhelm states, "The fact that the watchman is now friendly in-

[9] Donald Davie, *Ezra Pound: Poet as Sculptor* (New York, 1964), p. 112.
[10] *Ibid.*, p. 114.

126

forms us of the strongly positive values that secular love
. . . has now acquired."[11] The conflicting views of the
watchman and the lover concerning the value of the
sensual experience create a source of tension in the poem.

Pound had translated this poem by Giraut de Bornelh
quite literally in *The Spirit of Romance*. There the first
stanza reads:

> King Glorious, true light and clarity,
> God powerful, Lord if it pleaseth Thee
> To my companion be thou faithful aid,
> Him have I seen not since the night came on,
> And straightway comes the dawn.   (*SR*, 51)

In this version Pound makes no attempt to retain the
rhyme scheme (aabb and the refrain "et ades sera l'alba"),
but is content with presenting an "exegetic" translation.
The fusion of religious and secular imagery, which we
noticed in our earlier consideration of the *alba*, is quite
striking here: as Wilhelm states, the watchman "implores
Christ's help in this love-vigil without any apparent feel-
ing of conflict, as if it were perfectly natural for the
Christian God of Love to assume the practical functions
of pagan Amor."[12] Pound underlines this in his new ver-
sion, partly through his radical change of diction:

> O plasmatour and true celestial light,
> Lord powerful, engirdlèd all with might,
> Give my good-fellow aid in fools' despite
> Who stirs not forth this night,
> And day comes on. (*P*, 172)

The watchman's view of his friend's love is qualified
throughout this new version. He refers to his friend's
lovemaking as "fools' despite" and later he jocularly calls

[11] Wilhelm, *The Cruelest Month*, p. 198.
[12] *Ibid.*

127

his friend "Old swenken." Thus, Pound has him mock his friend's love—something he does not do in the Provençal.

Generally speaking, the tone throughout is much more familiar and less serious than in either the Provençal or the earlier translation. In the original version the watchman addresses his friend (at the beginning of stanzas 2-6) as "Bel companho" ("handsome" or "upright companion"), but Pound alters this radically:

"Sst! my good fellow . . ." (Stanza 2)
"Hi! Harry, hear me . . ." (Stanza 3)
"Come now! Old swenkin!" (Stanza 4)

In stanzas 2-6, where the watchman speaks directly to his friend and warns him of the end of night, Pound condenses the stanza from five to four lines. The lines most consistently dropped are those which develop the faithfulness of the watchman. The following lines (from the 1910 version) are deleted:

And I fear lest the "jealous" assail you . . .
　　(Stanza 3)
Know if I am a faithful messanger . . .
　　(Stanza 4)
"Bel Companho," since I left you
I have not slept nor moved from my knees . . .
　　(Stanza 5)
Since then I have watched all night through
　until the day . . .
　　(Stanza 6)

The effect of this is to diminish the stature of the watchman by de-emphasizing his close relationship with his friend. Deletion is not the only means by which Pound achieves this: he changes the fourth line of stanza 5 with a similar result. In the early version it reads: "That he give you back to me for loyal friendship," which Pound has changed to "To bring thee safe back, my companion." The importance of their friendship is simply not stressed in the new version. As a result, the watchman is a rather neutral character, and consequently we are less moved by his criticism of his friend's activity.

The final stanza, of doubtful authenticity, is unnecessary both in Pound's early version and in the Provençal where, as Wilhelm states, the "reply is fully evident in the interior dialectic of the poem."[13] It is, however, of considerable importance in the new translation, as a comparison of the two indicates:

Fair, sweet companion, I am in such rich delight
That I wish there should come never dawn nor day
For the noblest that was ever born of mother
I hold and embrace, so that I scarcely heed
The jealous fool or the dawn.

[1910]

"Wait, my good fellow. For such joy I take
With her venust and noblest to my make
To hold embracèd, and will not her forsake
For yammer of the cuckold,
Though day break."

[1918]

"Scarcely" is an important word in the first version: the lover realizes that his love will be terminated by the dawn, and he regretfully accepts this. In the second version, however, the lover asks his friend to wait, for he

13 *Ibid.*, p. 200.

refuses to part with his love. He is determined to make every effort to retain his moment of ecstasy, although the seriousness of his attempt is slightly undercut by his jocularity. Still, because of Pound's changes, the reader tends to sympathize more with the lover than in the earlier version, and this love is exalted over the petty concerns of his friend.

"Avril," the next poem in this sequence, is a translation of Guilhem de Peitieus' "Ab la dolchor del temps novel"; it shows the suffering of a lover who expects things to turn in his favor. It is the earliest example in Provençal of a poem with a spring opening, and the background of the season creates an ironic tension between the ideal (which the poet seeks) and the actual.

The poem has an interesting logic to it. The opening stanza presents the birds happily singing and, by extension, mating: should not man follow their example?

> When the springtime is sweet
> And the birds repeat
> Their new song in the leaves.
> 'Tis meet
> A man go where he will. (*P*, 173)

As in the preceding poem, Pound has adapted a rather flexible stanza, varying in length from five to six lines, with each line having from two to eleven feet. In the Provençal we find a fixed stanza of six octosyllabic lines, with a rhyme scheme of aabcbc, changing in the third stanza to bbcaca.

Pound has altered the meaning of this stanza somewhat, especially in the last two lines. In the Provençal, they read: "Then it is good that one enjoys / That which he longs for most," indicating the object of the speaker's search more specifically than in Pound's version, which is rather vague.

In the second stanza the lover has a setback, for he receives no word from his beloved, either of encouragement or of discouragement. The contrast between his state and the gay mood of the birds begins to be felt. Again, Pound changes the Provençal to make it more general. Where it reads "Nor dare I advance / Until I know if the end / Is what I ask for," he writes "Defeat / Or luck I must have my fill." Pound's speaker shows a determination to go ahead regardless of the consequences, much like the determination shown by the lover in the previous *alba*.

The remaining stanzas are of six lines each, and drop the pattern established by the first two stanzas. A note of hope is introduced in stanza 3, in an image which Dante later developed in the *Inferno* (II, 127-130):[14] like the branch of the hawthorne, which suffers during the winter night, only to bloom again in spring, so will his love be revived in this "sweet season." With such assurance he recalls one of those moments which Pound praises so highly:

> I remember the young day
> When we set strife away,
> And she gave me such gesning,
> Her love and her ring:
> God grant I die not by any man's stroke
> 'Till I have my hand 'neath her cloak.

The "young day" ("un mati") is the time of the *alba* as well, a sacred time for Pound. "Gesning" is a rather unfortunate choice here, probably determined by Pound's

14 Noted in *Ibid.*, p. 209.

desire for a rhyme. The Provençal is quite simple and clear: "E que·m donet un don tan gran" ("And she gave me a gift so great"). In spite of this, the stanza is successful, and it does show that what the speaker is longing for is based in sexual experience.

The final stanza maintains the concreteness of the sexual experience against the idle gossip of the boasters who lack such experience:

> I care not for their clamour
> Who have come between me and my charmer,
> For I know how words run loose,
> Big talk and little use.
> Spoilers of pleasure,
> We take their measure.

In the original there is a play on the *senhal*, "Bon Vezi" ("Good Neighbor"), which is lost by translating it as "charmer." However, lines three to five are an absolutely brilliant rendition of the Provençal. His final line is also good, although it lacks the concrete sexual imagery of the Provençal, which reads:

> Nos n'avem la pessa e·l coultel.[15]
> [We have the meat and the knife.]

"Avril," then, presents another example of the lover who is determined to proceed in spite of the obstacles that beset him. Once again, we see the importance of memory, and its ability to preserve moments that sustain one when the beloved is absent.

"Descant on a Theme by Cerclamon" also presents a speaker who is thwarted by *Amor* in the present, and who must rely on recollection and optimistic determina-

[15] Text in Appel, *Provenzalische Chrestomathie*, p. 51.

tion for strength. It is the major poem in the sequence, and the one that Pound considered most successful. Although based on Cercamon's poem, "Quant l'aura doussa s'amarzis," Pound has rearranged, condensed, expanded, and repeated the materials of Cercamon's poem. As a result, it is the freest version in the series. Here the typographical experimentation reaches a peak, as Pound strives to reproduce the musicality of the poet's speech.

The first stanza begins mournfully with a reference to autumn:

> When the sweet air goes bitter,
> And the cold birds twitter
> Where the leaf falls from the twig,
> I sough and sing
>
>> that Love goes out
>> Leaving me no power to hold him.
>>
>> (P, 174)

Here too the season plays an important role, and the mood is not unlike that of "Canzon: The Yearly Slain," where the death of the season corresponds to a defeat for the lover. Pound's version, however, is much bleaker than the original:

> Quant l'aura doussa s'amarzis
> E·l fuelha chai de su·l verjan
> E l'auzelh chanjan lor latis,
> Et ieu de sai sospir e chan
> D'Amor que·m te lassat e pres.
> Et encar non l'aic en poder.[16]
>
> [When the sweet wind becomes bitter
> And the leaf falls from the branch

16 Text in J. M. L. Dejeanne, "Le Troubadour Cercamon," *Annales du Midi*, xvi, 65 (Jan. 1905), p. 38.

And the birds sing in their language
And here I sigh and sing
Because of Love which holds me bound and taken.
For I never had him in my power.]

Pound has emphasized the bitterness of the season by add-
ing "cold" and by translating "sing" as "twitter." More
important, Pound has altered the nature of love as it is
presented here. In Cercamon's poem, there is a struggle
between love and the speaker. Love has the speaker
"bound and taken," simply because the speaker has not
been able to conquer love. The notion of a struggle be-
tween love and the speaker is continued in the second
stanza of the Provençal:

Las! qu'ieu d'Amor non si conquis
Mas las trebalhas e l'afan . . .

[Alas! that I only conquered
The pain and the sorrow of Love . . .]

In Pound's version this struggle does not exist: Love has
fled from this world ("Love goes out") and thus the
speaker is without any power whatsoever. Pound seems
to conceive of love as a force one can only work with,
rather than a force one struggles against. Thus, when
Amor is absent, one can have no success with his beloved.

The third stanza of Pound's version (stanza 4 in the
original) presents a vision of this beloved developed in
terms of the light imagery of the Tuscan poets. Let us
first look at the Provençal:

Tota la gensor qu'anc hom vis
Encontra lieys no pretz un guan;
Quan totz lo segles brunezis,
Lay ou ylh es, aqui resplan.

Dieus mi respieyt tro qu·ieu l'agues
O qu'ieu la vej'anar jazer.

[All the most beautiful that man ever saw
Compared to her, I value not so much as a
    glove:
When all the world darkens
There where she is, it becomes radiant.
God give me rest until I have her,
Or until I see her go to bed.]

In both of Pound's versions the radiance of the woman
becomes the focal point of the stanza. The first version
(stanza 3), however, emphasizes the last two lines of the
Provençal:

With the noblest that stands in men's sight,
If all the world be in despite
        I care not a glove.
Where my love is, there is a glitter of sun;
God give me life, and let my course run

        'Till I have her I love
        To lie with and prove.   (*P*, 174)

Again, Pound's speaker shows a greater determination to
pursue the lady than does the speaker in the original.

The remaining stanzas show the torment of the lover,
who can be saved only by the lady he admires. However,
she shows no inclination to help him:

I am gone from one joy,
From one I loved never so much,
        She by one touch
        Reft me away;
        So doth bewilder me
        I can not say my say

> nor my desire,
> And when she looks on me
> It seems to me
>
> I lose all wit and sense.
>
> (*P*, 176)

Although he appears unable to have any relationship with his beloved, she remains an ideal who guides and inspires him. He concludes the poem by repeating the third stanza in a different version, thus affirming his devotion to her:

> The noblest girls men love
> 'Gainst her I prize not as a glove
> Worn and old.
> Though the whole world run rack
> And go dark with cloud,
> Light is
> Where she stands,
> And a clamour loud
>
> in my ears.   (*P*, 176)

Regardless of what happens, the radiant light symbolizing the lady's *virtù* will sustain him.

"Vergier," the next poem in the series, is a new version of the *alba* Pound had translated as "Alba innominata."[17] As we have seen, the narrator frames the action in an opening stanza that establishes the tone and the setting, and in the closing stanza in which he condones the adulterous relationship he has just witnessed. In the four middle stanzas, a lady speaks of her relationship to her beloved, and of her desire that it not cease with the dawn. Pound alters this scheme in his new version, by having the lady's lover speak in the last two stanzas. Although

---

[17] See Chapter I, pp. 12-16.

this does not significantly change the outcome of the poem (adulterous love is accepted in both versions), it does broaden the perspective.

The most significant difference between the two versions is in the language. Here Pound has retained the original rhyme scheme, and eliminated the Pre-Raphaelite and *fin-de-siècle* mannerisms that filled the earlier version. The language of the new poem has a deft movement that is quite extraordinary, as a comparison of the final stanza of the two versions indicates:

> Fair is this damsel and right courteous,
> And many watch her beauty's gracious way.
> Her heart toward love is no wise traitorous.
> Ah God! Ah God! That dawns should come so soon!
> > [1909]

> *Venust the lady, and none lovelier,*
> *For her great beauty, many men look on her,*
> *Out of my love will her heart not stir.*
> *By God! how swift the night.*
> > *And day comes on.*
> > [1918]

The final line, which is choppy and languorous in the early version, has a fluidity of movement here surpassing even the Provençal. Pound's archaisms, such as "plasmatour" and "venust," while a little recherché, are none the less new constructions, which the earlier archaisms ("right courteous" and "beauty's gracious way") were not. Thus, we actively respond to them, as we are unable to do with a language to which we are preconditioned.

The final poem in the sequence, "I only, and who elrische pain support," is the version of "Sols sui" which we considered in the preceding chapter.[18] After republishing it with the other Daniel translations in *Instigations*, Pound dropped it from the sequence. As we have seen, it deals with loss or separation, a persistent theme of "Homage à la Langue d'Oc." In spite of the separation, the speaker's lady remains a paragon of virtue, and his constant source of inspiration:

> Measure and sense to mate,
> Youth and beauty learnèd in all delight,
> Gentrice did nurse her up, and so advance
> Her fair beyond all reach of evil name,
> To clear her worth, no shadow hath oppresst it.

$(T, 179)$

Taken as a whole, this sequence affirms the transitory nature of the moment of bliss between lovers. In spite of the separation or loss that inevitably follows this, the lover remains perennially optimistic, determined, and faithful to the memory of his beloved, whom he reveres above everything else. She represents an ideal of perfection towards which he must strive. This is quite consistent with the Neo-Platonic idealization of love examined in Chapter III, as well as with the values Pound emphasized in his early personae and translations. What is significant here is that Pound's final work dealing exclusively with Provence considers only its love ethic. The reasons for Pound's difficulty in finding a language become clear at last. The spirit of Provence, as he interprets it, is "archaic" inasmuch as its values and sensibility do not function effectively in the modern world. Love has become de-

[18] Chapter IV, pp. 111-114.

based (see the images of *fals' amors* in *The Cantos*, and the association there between this love and prostitution) and we have lost the mystical reverence for *Amor* that permeated the medieval world. Consequently, *Amor* cannot adequately be described in nineteenth or twentieth century English, and a new language must be created. The modern, ironic diction of "Moeurs Contemporains" and *Homage to Sextus Propertius* is simply not applicable to *fin' amors*. Although Pound's language in "Homage à la Langue d'Oc" is still not satisfactory, he is clearly progressing towards a solution to this problem.

In *The Cantos* Pound finally succeeds in creating such a language, clearly demonstrated in "Canto XXXVI," a retranslation of "Donna mi prega." It is an archaic language that manages to avoid the grotesque terminology of "Homage à la Langue d'Oc," while retaining the flavor of the past. Pound uses this language when he wishes to evoke or describe *fin' amors* and the sensibility that produced it. The final lines of his translation of "Donna mi prega" in "Canto XXXVI," which could easily be applied to Pound's total *oeuvre*, are a beautiful example of this:

> Go, song, surely thou mayest
> Whither it please thee
> For so art thou ornate that thy reasons
> Shall be praised from thy understanders,
> With others hast thou no will to make company.

Chapter VI

THE PERMANENCE OF PROVENCE

What thou lovest well remains,
> the rest is dross
What thou lov'st well shall not be reft from thee
What thou lov'st well is thy true heritage . . .
"Canto LXXXI"

THROUGHOUT *The Cantos*, from the first version of "Canto I" (June, 1917), to the "Notes for Canto CXVII et seq." (1968), Pound has continually made use of Provençal material, a fact obvious to even the most cursory reader of his work. Several important questions arise regarding the use of Provençal materials in *The Cantos*: (1) Does Pound continue to develop the themes of this material in the ways we have already witnessed? (2) In what way (if any) does the technique of *The Cantos* continue the experimentation and developments of the early work? (3) Does this material help to provide an ordering structure for *The Cantos*? Answers to these questions should indicate the importance of Pound's work with Provence in terms of his total *oeuvre*, of which *The Cantos* are obviously a significant part.

One of Pound's early goals, in the character studies and translations of *Personae* (1909) and *Exultations* (1909), was to recreate successfully a historical period. In the epigraph to "Sestina: Altaforte" he poses a question that he would certainly answer in the affirmative: "Have I dug him [Bertran de Born] up again?" In the early works he is determined to show that he can revive the past, and succeed in making the Provençal poets his con- temporaries. Through his development of the persona in such poems as "Marvoil," "Piere Vidal Old," "Na Audi- art," and "Sestina: Altaforte," Pound is able to penetrate an alien sensibility and make it his own, thereby becom- ing a spokesman for the persona. The technique of the persona is one that he uses to great advantage in *The Can- tos.* Implicit in his treatment of the past, both in the early poems and *The Cantos*, is his recognition of the perma- nence of the values represented by each historical figure and the relevance of these values to the contemporary world. Each historical character is chosen because he em- bodies certain values that Pound finds attractive: taken together, they indicate why Provence has exerted such an appeal for him.

The values Pound attributes to the culture of Provence in his earliest poems remain constant in his treatment of this material in *The Cantos.* The significant change here is in the presentation, for in *The Cantos* only a few sugges- tive and evocative details are given, and the reader is left to fill in the background and ascertain the significance of this material for himself. A good example of this is Pound's treatment of Peire Vidal, first in "Piere Vidal Old" and later in "Canto IV." "Piere Vidal Old" pre- sents Vidal's recreation, through memory, of the ex- perience that gave his madness meaning—his seduction

141

of Na Loba. He recounts the experience in detail, and by going over it he is able to reexperience his metamorphosis and participate once more in the natural universe of which he once was a part. Our knowledge of Pound's interpretation of that experience is necessary if we are to understand his use of Vidal in "Canto IV":

> Actaeon . . .
>   and a valley,
> The valley is thick with leaves, with leaves, the trees,
> The sunlight glitters, glitters a-top,
> Like a fish-scale roof,
>   Like the church roof in Poictiers
> If it were gold.
>   Beneath it, beneath it
> Not a ray, not a slivver, not a spare disc of sunlight
> Flaking the black, soft water;
> Bathing the body of nymphs, of nymphs, and Diana,
> Nymphs, white-gathered about her, and the air, air,
> Shaking, air alight with the goddess,
>   fanning their hair in the dark,
> Lifting, lifting and waffing:
> Ivory dipping in silver,
>   Shadow'd, o'ershadow'd
> Ivory dipping in silver,
> Not a splotch, not a lost shatter of sunlight.
> Then Actaeon: Vidal,
> Vidal. It is old Vidal speaking,
>   stumbling along in the wood,
> Not a patch, not a lost shimmer of sunlight,
>   the pale hair of the goddess.
>
> The dogs leap on Actaeon,
>   'Hither, hither, Actaeon,'
> Spotted stag of the wood;

Gold, gold, a sheaf of hair,
    Thick like a wheat swath,
Blaze, blaze in the sun,
    The dogs leap on Actaeon.
Stumbling, stumbling along in the wood,
Muttering, muttering Ovid:
    'Pergusa . . . pool . . . pool . . . Gargaphia,
Pool . . . pool of Salmacis.'
    The empty armour shakes as the cygnet moves.

Pound has juxtaposed the legend of Actaeon and Diana with the legendary account of Vidal. Although the Vidal material occupies only a few lines, it illuminates the other legend quite successfully. Both legends deal with metamorphosis, resulting from a mystical perception of great intensity. In the case of Actaeon, this is the moment at which he perceives Diana bathing with the

Nymphs, white-gathered about her, and the air, air,
Shaking, air alight with the goddess,
    fanning their hair in the dark.

Because of her anger at Actaeon for having seen her, Diana has him turned into a stag, who is hunted and ultimately killed by his own dogs.

Vidal, however, wills his own metamorphosis. What is significant in the parallel is that both result from a moment of intense perception (such as that described in "Piere Vidal Old"), and both Vidal and Actaeon symbolize man's connection with the "vital universe," discussed in Chapter II. This connection permits both Vidal and Actaeon to experience what George Dekker has called "an ecstatic vision of creativity"[1] in the passage that immediately follows:

[1] Dekker, *Sailing After Knowledge*, p. 57.

143

Thus the light rains, thus pours, *e lo soleils plovil*
The liquid and rushing crystal
   beneath the knees of the gods.
Ply over ply, thin glitter of water;
Brook film bearing white petals.
The pines at Takasago
   grow with the pines of Isé!
The water whirls up the bright pale sand in the
         spring's mouth
'Behold the Tree of the Visages!'
Forked branch-tips, flaming as if with lotus.
   Ply over ply
The shallow eddying fluid,
   beneath the knees of gods.

This passage, built around a line from Daniel's "Lancan son passat li giure," shows the connection of Eros and knowledge, a theme Pound has also developed in "The Flame." The sexual encounters of Vidal and Actaeon permit them to experience this revelatory intuition, although in both cases the cost is great.

Thus Pound's interpretation of Vidal's experience has not changed between the writing of "Piere Vidal Old" and "Canto IV." This is true of his use of Provençal material in general; consequently the early poems and prose writings can often serve as glosses on passages in *The Cantos*. The presentation has obviously changed, and Pound now expects us to recognize the significance of Vidal without having to relate the experience in its entirety. Each fragment in *The Cantos* is meant to evoke the larger work of which it is a part, with its accretions of historical and literary meaning. Thus, to take another example, when Pound quotes part of a line from the *planh* of Bertran de Born in *The Pisan Cantos* (LXXX and

LXXXIV), the reader is meant to think not only of the historical events surrounding the writing of the poem, but also of the qualities epitomized by the "young English King." These, of course, are the qualities that Pound had stressed in his early translation of this poem.

The values which Pound assigns to the personae of his early poems and translations remain fairly constant in *The Cantos*, and he continues to use historical material in much the same way. Pound also employs many of the themes he had developed in his treatment of troubadour poetry, especially the concept of love discussed in Chapter III. *Fin' amors* becomes the cornerstone of Pound's love ethic, and he continues to depict it through images of radiant light (for example, in the passage beginning with the line from Daniel quoted above). Throughout *The Cantos* this concept of love is juxtaposed with the *mal' amors* of "Canzon: The Yearly Slain." The most elaborate exposition of *fin' amors* in *The Cantos* occurs in "Canto XXXVI." This canto contains a new translation of Cavalcanti's "Donna mi prega," one of the most detailed expositions *fin' amors* in medieval poetry. It is an elaboration of the Provençal love ethic, and Pound underscores the relationship of this work to Provençal poetry by his references to the troubadours in the second half of the canto. The love ethic expressed here becomes a permanent part of Pound's work, and he continues to build upon it throughout *The Cantos*.

"Provincia Deserta" (March 1915) and "Near Perigord" (December 1915), are an important step beyond Pound's early poetry, for they present thematic and technical developments that Pound was able to utilize in *The Cantos*. "Provincia Deserta" is a meditation on the possibilities of reviving history through the evocation of an area, the personal involvement in this setting, and the resuscitation of historical characters. "Near Perigord" considers these same issues in a more complex form. Like "Marvoil," "Piere Vidal Old," and "Sestina: Altaforte," it attempts to solve the "riddle" of the character's personality that is concealed by his lyrics and *vida*. The interrogatory technique developed in this poem, in which Pound questions the validity of both historical "fact" and his own "fictions," reappears often in *The Cantos*. A good example of this is a passage concerning Italian Renaissance history in "Canto v." Both Pound and Varchi, the historian, consider the motives behind the assassinations of Giovanni Borgia and Alessandro de Medici:

> But Varchi of Florence,
> Steeped in a different year, and pondering Brutus,
> Then "Σίγα μαλ' αὖθις δευτέραν!
> "Dog-eye!!" (to Alessandro)
>   "Whether for love of Florence," Varchi
>   leaves it,
> Saying "I saw the man, came up with him at Venice,
> "I, one wanting the facts,
> "And no mean labour . . . Or for a privy spite?"

This is obviously the technique of "Near Perigord," where alternative responses are given to each question. Pound's material there, as in *The Cantos*, is a collection of historical and fictional fragments ("a broken bundle of mirrors") that can be given unity only by the artist.

The poem upon which "Near Perigord" is based, "Dompna Pois," illuminates another important aspect of *The Cantos*: Pound's method of presentation, especially as it applies to his epic hero. In the epigraph preceding "Na Audiart," Pound speaks of "Dompna Pois" as a poem in which the artist creates " 'Una dompna soiseubuda' a borrowed lady or as the Italians translated it 'Una donna ideale' " (P, 8). In our discussion of that poem we noticed that it symbolized Pound's poetic method (the creation of an ideal through the accumulation of fragments); this is also the method of *The Cantos*. Pound later called this the "ideogrammatic method," but he discovered it in Provence long before he came across the Fenollosa manuscripts. Pound's epic hero can also be defined in these terms, for he is really "un om soiseubut," a "borrowed" (and "ideal") man, the composite *persona* who undergoes a series of significant metamorphoses. When considered in this context, the similarities of the individual personae of *The Cantos* become quite apparent.

Having considered the ways in which the themes and techniques of Pound's early verse are developed in *The Cantos*, we should now determine whether this material provides any ordering structure for *The Cantos*. Both "Provincia Deserta" and "Near Perigord" show ways of structuring Provençal material in a poem of some length, and both are concerned with resuscitating and interpreting the past. "Near Perigord" does develop a technique that many of the individual cantos employ, but its form is not sufficiently flexible for a poem of the length of *The Cantos*. Pound turned instead to Browning's *Sordello*, another poetic recreation of Provence that he thought might provide a model for the type of work he intended to do in *The Cantos*.

In his detailed consideration of "Pound's Revision of Cantos I-III," John L. Foster has noted the pervading influence of Browning: "Basically, these cantos are a colloquy with Browning in which Pound seeks illumination concerning two problems: the form his own work is to

147

take, coming as it does after Browning's *Sordello*, and the possibility of recovering the living essence of the past— of reviving it, truly making it new, and using it as a valid standard by which to judge the present."[2] The question of form had been preoccupying Pound for a long time. In his *Paris Review* interview of 1962, he spoke of this: "I began the *Cantos* about 1904, I suppose. I had various schemes, starting in 1904 or 1905. The problem was to get a form—something elastic enough to take the necessary material. It had to be a form that wouldn't exclude something merely because it didn't fit."[3] Pound addresses Browning in the first published version of "Canto I," and asks him what form he can utilize, now that *Sordello* has exhausted certain possibilities:

> Hang it all, there can be but one *Sordello*!
> But say I want to, say I take your whole
>   bag of tricks,
> Let in your quirks and tweeks, and say the
>   thing's an art form,
> Your *Sordello*, and that the modern world
> Needs such a rag-bag to stuff all its thought
>   in . . .
>
> So you worked out new form, the meditative,
> Semi-dramatic, semi-epic story,
> And we will say: What's left for me to do?
> Whom shall I conjure up; who's my Sordello,
> My pre-Daun Chaucer, pre-Boccacio,
>   As you have done pre-Dante?
> Whom shall I hang my shimmering garment on;

    [2] John L. Foster, "Pound's Revision of Cantos I-III," *Modern Philology*, LXIII (1966), p. 237.
    [3] *Ibid.*, p. 236. See also Van Wyck Brooks, ed., *Writers at Work: The Paris Review Interviews* (New York, 1963), p. 38.

Who wear my feathery mantle, *hagoromo*;
Whom set to dazzle the serious future ages?[4]

Another problem, closely related to the question of form, is the choice of epic hero ("who's my Sordello"). These early cantos show Pound's self-conscious search for answers to these problems.

Pound tries a "rag-bag" form like *Sordello*, and finds Browning's method inapplicable. For one thing, the age has changed, and the beliefs of Browning's time no longer sustain it:

You had one whole man?
And I have many fragments, less worth? Less worth?
Ah, had you quite my age, quite such a beastly
and cantankerous age?
You had some basis, had some set belief.
Am I let preach? Has it a place in music?

The individual, like his age, has become fragmented, and thus Pound finds it difficult to select a single persona upon whom to hang his "shimmering garment":

Not Arnaut, not De Born, not Uc St. Circ who
has writ out the stories.

Ultimately, as we have seen, Pound will settle upon an "om soiseubut" for his hero, but at this date (c. 1917) he can find neither a hero nor a form. However, he does affirm the validity and relevance of his poetic recreations of history. As Foster states: "The bulk of the material in the first two Cantos of this version . . . concerns the effectiveness of the past. From doubt ('What have I of this life?') Pound moves to an affirmation, one based

---

[4] Ezra Pound, "Three Cantos, I," *Poetry*, X (June 1917), pp. 113-121.

upon his intuition that some sort of permanence does exist in the universe."[5] This is the "permanent basis in humanity" (*SR*, 92) that permits one to consider historical figures as contemporaries. Of course Pound does not limit himself to Provençal history, but in his early use of Provençal material he has developed a method for recreating the historical past, and he continues to use this method in *The Cantos*.

By 1923 Pound had solved the problem of form by adopting the ideogrammatic method, which, as we have seen, is similar to the method of "Dompna Pois." He also utilizes the "polyphonic rhyme" of Daniel, "modified and elaborated as befits its application to a structure of a magnitude Arnaut never envisaged."[6] The "colloquy with Browning" has become reduced to the lines with which "Canto II" opens:

> Hang it all, Robert Browning,
>   there can be but the one 'Sordello.'
> But Sordello, and my Sordello?
> Lo Sordels si fo di Mantovana.

Pound accepts the fact that Browning's poem is a unique artistic creation that cannot be duplicated ("there can be but the one 'Sordello' "), but he also recognizes that there can be any number of individual Sordellos—his, Browning's, and the historical Sordello being but three of the many possibilities. In the revised version of "Cantos I-III" there is less Provençal material, and the Ulysses episode achieves greater prominence. As *The Cantos* developed it became increasingly clear that no single cultural framework could be large enough to encompass such an ambitious work. "Oh, we have worlds enough, and brave

---

[5] Foster, "Pound's Revision of Cantos I-III," pp. 238-239.
[6] Kenner, "Horizontal Chords," p. 231.

décors," Pound states in the first version of "Canto I," and Provence has remained an important world among the many included in *The Cantos*. In the broad philosophical framework of *The Cantos*, the medieval world that began in Provence becomes the cornerstone of Pound's Paradise: it is a brilliantly unified world against which he can contrast the chaos of contemporary civilization. Equally important is the fact that Pound has discovered ways of dealing with historical material through his work with Provençal poetry that have proved useful in *The Cantos*. Eliot has cited Pound as the introducer of Chinese poetry to the modern world, and much the same could be said of his work with the culture of Provence: he has "made it new," and as a result it has become a permanent part of our "true heritage."

INDEX

153

Princeton Essays in Literature

The Orbit of Thomas Mann. By Erich Kahler

On Four Modern Humanists: Hofmannsthal, Gundolf, Curtius, Kantorowicz. Edited by Arthur R. Evans, Jr.

Flaubert and Joyce: The Rite of Fiction. By Richard Cross

A Stage for Poets: Studies in the Theatre of Hugo and Musset. By Charles Affron

Hofmannsthal's Novel "Andreas." By David H. Miles

Kazantzakis and the Linguistic Revolution in Greek Literature. By Peter Bien

Modern Greek Writers. Edited by Edmund Keeley and Peter Bien

On Gide's Prométhée: Private Myth and Public Mystification. By Kurt Weinberg

The Inner Theatre of Recent French Poetry. By Mary Ann Caws

Wallace Stevens and the Symbolist Imagination. By M. Benamou

Cervantes' Christian Romance: A Study of "Persiles y Sigismunda." By Alban K. Forcione

The Prison-House of Language: A Critical Account of Structuralism and Russian Formalism. By Fredric Jameson

Ezra Pound and the Troubadour Tradition. By Stuart Y. McDougal

Wallace Stevens: Imagination and Faith. By Adalaide Kirby Morris

The Art of Medieval Arabic Literature. By Andras Hamori